BERWICK
TO
ST. BOSWELLS
VIA KELSO

INCLUDING THE JEDBURGH BRANCH

Roger Darsley & Dennis Lovett
Series Editor Vic Mitchell

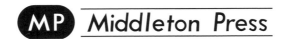

Readers of this book may be interested in the following societies:

North Eastern Railway Association
c/o K Richardson, Membership Secretary,
7, Grenadier Drive,
Northallerton,
DL6 1SB
www.ner.org.uk

North British Railway Study Group
c/o R.W.Lynn,
2, Brecken Court, Saltwell Road South,
Low Fell, Gateshead,
NE9 6EY
www.nbrstudygroup.co.uk

Published May 2015
First reprint January 2016

ISBN 978 1 908174 75 8

© Middleton Press, 2015

Design Deborah Esher

Published by
   Middleton Press
   Easebourne Lane
   Midhurst
   West Sussex
   GU29 9AZ
Tel: 01730 813169
Email: info@middletonpress.co.uk
www.middletonpress.co.uk

Printed in the United Kingdom by Henry Ling Limited, at the Dorset Press, Dorchester, DT1 1HD

INDEX

ACKNOWLEDGEMENTS

We are grateful for the assistance received from many of those mentioned in the photographic credits and also to G.Beecroft, M.Christensen (World War Two Study Group), G.Croughton, N.Langridge, J.P.McCrickard, A.P.McLean, V.Mitchell, J.W.Yellowlees (First ScotRail) and Mrs N.Darsley.

I.   The route in 1948 is highlighted in this map showing its relevance to the other lines in the Borders. (A.E.Young)

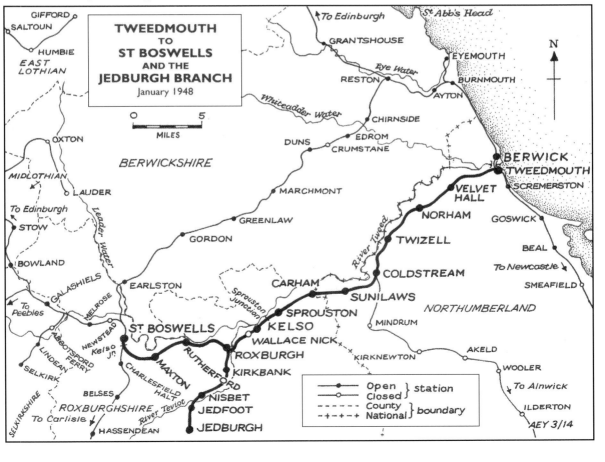

GEOGRAPHICAL SETTING

This line between Berwick and St. Boswells is sometimes referred to as the Tweed Valley line because it follows the south bank of the River Tweed closely for most of its route. The catchment of the River Tweed is the horseshoe of hills formed by the Southern Uplands and the Cheviot Hills. Downstream of St. Boswells, the Tweed enters the broad rolling plain of the Merse of Berwickshire. Thick layers of glacial deposits cover the Old Red Sandstone bedrock giving fertile clay loams to support the agriculture of the Merse. In most places the actual river valley is narrow but at Kelso and Coldstream there are alluvial expanses with sand and gravel.

On leaving Berwick, Kelso line trains crossed the River Tweed by the Royal Border Bridge and the East Coast Main Line to access Tweedmouth on the opposite side of the river. Before 1482 the River Tweed was the border separating Scotland and England but the Border today is Lamberton, 2½ miles north of Tweedmouth. The junction for the line to Kelso (and also to Alnwick) was north west of the station and could only be accessed from the south. This required the locomotives to run around their train before leaving the East Coast Main Line to head off towards the west and Kelso.

Coldstream, the only major town on the North Eastern section of the route was denied direct access to the railway by local landowners who kept it out of the town. Coldstream, although in Scotland, had to rely on its station being in England on the south side of the river in the village of Cornhill-on-Tweed. Shortly after leaving Coldstream station, the Alnwick line (opened in 1887) branched off from the Kelso line reaching Alnwick via Wooler.

The English village of Carham had the station bearing its name on the Scottish side of the Border. The railway was also denied access to Kelso which lies some 142ft above sea level on the north bank of the Tweed. The town was linked to its railway station at Maxwellhaugh, on the south bank, by Rennie's road bridge over the River Tweed. This mirrored the situation at Coldstream, although in this case at least the town and station are in the same country!

Shortly before entering Roxburgh the line crossed the steep sided valley of the River Teviot on a high viaduct and then ran through rich arable farm land between Roxburgh and Maxton. The Teviot joins the Tweed in Kelso. At Kelso Junction, just south of St. Boswells station, the line from Berwick joined the Waverley Route for the short run into St. Boswells station where trains terminated. Maps are 20 inches to 1 mile, with north at the top, if appropriate, unless otherwise stated.

The Jedburgh line ran from Roxburgh, along the west bank of the Teviot (via Kirkbank and Nisbet). At Jedfoot it then followed the west bank of the Jed Water to the northern outskirts of the town.

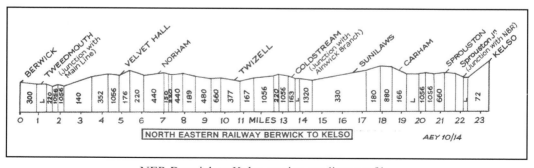

NER Berwick to Kelso section gradient profile.

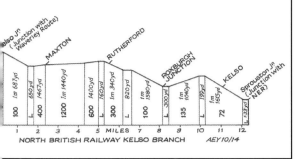

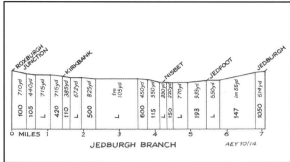

NBR St. Boswells to Kelso section gradient profile.   NBR Jedburgh branch gradient profile.

HISTORICAL BACKGROUND

An attempt to build a line to Kelso was first mooted as early as 1809 when railways were very much in their infancy. The Berwick & Kelso Railway planned to build a 22 mile line from Spittal (near Berwick) to Kelso but the plans were abandoned in 1827 having never really got off the ground. An attempt to resurrect it in 1836 also came to nothing. These early efforts did involve the famous civil engineers, John Rennie and Thomas Telford.

A further link to Kelso was mooted by the Caledonian Railway who were keen to penetrate North British territory. The Caledonian Extension Railway in 1845 proposed a 104 mile line from Ayr to Berwick-upon-Tweed running via Muirkirk, Biggar, Stobo, Peebles, Innerleithen, Galashiels, Melrose and Kelso. These plans came to nothing, although eventually all the places mentioned would be rail served, but the Caledonian failed to penetrate any further than Peebles into the North British stronghold in South East Scotland.

The Newcastle & Berwick Railway was the first to actually reach the area. Its own line was authorised from Tweedmouth, near Berwick-upon-Tweed, in 1845 and terminated initially at Sprouston some 1½ miles short of Kelso. The Newcastle & Berwick became the York Berwick & Newcastle Railway on 9th August 1847 which, in turn, would become part of the new North Eastern Railway on 31st July 1854. The double track line from Tweedmouth opened to Sprouston on 27th July 1849. The 23½ mile line was extended to Kelso two years later on 1st June 1851 to join up with the North British line from St. Boswells at Mellendean Farm. This resulted in the only instance of an English company owning stations at Carham and Sprouston in Scotland. Carham is further unique in that the village itself is within England but its station was across the border in Scotland.

The Edinburgh & Hawick Railway was planned as a single track extension to the Edinburgh & Dalkeith railway to the 4ft 6ins Scotch gauge and gained Parliamentary approval in 1845. It utilised the existing Edinburgh & Dalkeith (opened in 1831) and the Marquess of Lothian's waggonway which opened in 1832. Before work began, the new Edinburgh & Hawick Railway was acquired by the North British Railway (NBR) with the route being upgraded to double track and built to the British Standard Gauge of 4ft 8½ ins with the existing route converted accordingly. The line to Hawick reached St. Boswells in 1849.

Keen to serve other Border towns, the North British Railway Branch Line Act received approval on 26th June 1846 to build three lines radiating from the Waverley Route; from Galashiels to Selkirk, St. Boswells to Kelso and from Roxburgh to Jedburgh. At that time the North British was then converting the Hawick branch from the original Edinburgh & Dalkeith Railway 4ft 6ins line to standard gauge and the construction of the line south to Hawick which was later extended to Carlisle to become the Waverley Route. Of the three branch lines planned, it was the line to Kelso that would be built first.

The Duke of Roxburghe was not enthusiastic about the North British line reaching the town and this resulted in the line from St. Boswells initially terminating at Wallace Nick in January 1850 and Maxwellhaugh, on the south bank of the River Tweed opposite Kelso, the following year.

Eventually agreement was reached for the North British and York, Newcastle & Berwick lines to physically join, providing the ability to transfer passengers and goods between the two systems. The latter company reached agreement to operate into the NBR station at Kelso.

When the line from Tweedmouth became part of the North Eastern Railway in 1854, relationships between the two companies deteriorated. In order to reach Newcastle from its Hawick – Hexham line, the North British Railway had been forced to concede haulage of East Coast express passenger trains over its tracks between Berwick and Edinburgh to the North Eastern.

The Kelso line could have formed a useful through route between the two main lines at Berwick and St. Boswells. Instead of operating joint through trains the two companies operated their respective Kelso services as dedicated branch lines. Any passenger wishing to travel between Roxburgh and Berwick would have suffered a great deal of inconvenience as services between the two companies were uncoordinated. Lengthy changes at Kelso were the norm. Even when the two companies found themselves part of the same company (London & North Eastern Railway) in 1923, there was little improvement. Both lines were built as double track, but the St. Boswells to Kelso line was singled from 5th November 1933. Done in stages it was completed by 10th December 1933.

Shortly after nationalisation (1st January 1948) the newly-formed British Railways North Eastern Region took over the former LNER Scottish Area lines in England. In exchange, Carham and Sprouston were given to the newly-formed British Railways, Scottish Region.

It was only after nationalisation that the Kelso lines came into their own. This was not due to any reorganisation but out of necessity when floods brought chaos to most of the Borders infrastructure. The 6th August 1948 saw torrential downpours which continued for six days and nights. On the 12th August, the East Coast Main Line between Berwick and Dunbar was breached when the Rivers Eye and Tweed, already at flood level, rose to 20ft above normal levels resulting in 14 landslips and 11 damaged bridges, closing the route for 11 weeks and not allowing reopening until 25th October when all repairs had been completed.

During this time East Coast Main Line trains between Newcastle and Edinburgh were diverted with the Berwick to St. Boswells line playing a key role; the trains continuing to Edinburgh via the Waverley Route, which had itself been closed for a short period following the deluge. In order to accommodate the diverted trains the timetabled passenger service on the line was temporarily withdrawn. It was reinstated after the East Coast Main Line reopened between Berwick and Edinburgh on 1st November 1948.

By 1956 only Coldstream and Norham between Berwick and Kelso remained opened for passenger traffic. The line closed to passengers on 15th June 1964 and to goods between Tweedmouth and Kelso on 29th March 1965 and Kelso to St Boswells on 1st April 1968.

The line may well have survived that long due to the Cold War. It has been suggested that the Cheviots were being considered for a nuclear storage area close to Yetholm. This would have required rail access and consideration was given to using the Kelso line from either Tweedmouth or from St. Boswells via the then still open Waverley route. Although nothing came of the scheme, it resulted in the closure documents being restricted under the Government's 30 year rule.

When Penmanshiel Tunnel (between Grantshouse and Cockburnspath) collapsed on 17th March 1979 during major engineering work, there was no alternative but to resort to buses between Berwick and Dunbar along the A1 trunk road. The route that had kept open for diversions in 1948 was no longer an option – just a memory.

Jedburgh Branch

This branch was originally authorised along with the St. Boswells to Kelso line on 26th June 1846 but was not built. The Jedburgh Railway Company was authorised on 25th July 1855 to build this line and opened it on 17th July 1856. It was operated by the North British Railway from the start. On 3rd July 1860 the Jedburgh Railway Company was taken over by the NBR.

The seven mile long branch to Jedburgh left the Kelso line at Roxburgh Junction and followed the valleys of the Teviot and the Jed Water. It terminated ¾ miles north of the town centre to which it was linked by omnibus.

Like other lines in the Borders, the Jedburgh branch did not escape the floods of August 1948, with flooding taking place at Jedfoot. Commencing on the 6th August 1948 heavy rainfall resulted in the withdrawal of passenger trains on the Jedburgh branch from 13th August in order to create extra train paths on the Berwick-Kelso-St. Boswells line for diverted East Coast Express trains. Passenger services did not restart after this though the line remained open to goods traffic until 10th August 1964.

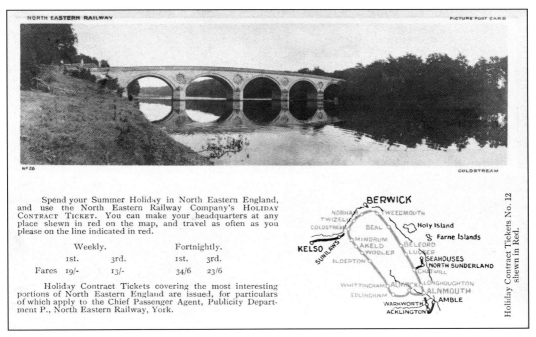

An NER postcard advertising the Holiday Contract tickets which provided a circular tour of North Northumberland including the Berwick - Coldstream section covered in this book. (J.Alsop coll.)

PASSENGER SERVICES

In 1849, the line from Tweedmouth was open to Sprouston with three trains each way and two on Sundays. The extension to Kelso was on 1st June 1851. The NBR line from St Boswells was under construction and finished to Kelso by 1851. The NBR Jedburgh branch opened in 1856. To get from Tweedmouth to Sprouston would have cost 4s, 1st class, or 1s.9d by government train - this was not cheap.

By 1895 the line was being worked as three branches, the two NBR branches working to Kelso with six trains each way with two on Sundays. The NER branch ran five trains each way from Berwick to Kelso plus two extra to Coldstream (though only one back). There were also two trains each way on Sundays. The different companies' timetables were not integrated.

This separate working of the branches continued even through LNER days. By 1922 St Boswells to Kelso had six trains in each direction. By 1935 the Jedburgh branch still had six trains but an extra two on Saturdays. Regular excursions on the lines brought longer trains with unusual locomotives, particularly those for the agricultural shows at Kelso. These came from Peebles, Hawick and Edinburgh. There were no specials from Berwick for these shows but extra coaches were put on the normal trains. In the Summer timetable from 1933 to 1939 there was a Sunday express from York to Edinburgh via Tweedbank, Kelso and St. Boswells, returning by the same route. There were also occasional military specials to Jedburgh for the Otterburn ranges. From time to time it was used as a diversionary route, when there was trouble on the East Coast Main Line or Waverley route, but mainly it served a rural economy.

It was only after nationalisation that the line was advertised as a through route between St Boswells and Berwick upon Tweed. In 1960, Berwick to St Boswells had two through trains but only the NER stations of Tweedmouth, Norham and Coldstream were served by train, with the other stations served by Scottish Omnibuses Ltd. Kelso to St Boswells had another four trains each way.

Passenger services ceased on the Jedburgh branch after the flood damage in 1948. The line was restored for goods traffic and was used for a yearly excursion from Jedburgh to Tweedmouth for the All Churches trip to Spittal Beach; 1000 people were taken by two class J37 0-6-0s double heading. St Boswells to Berwick passenger trains lasted until June 1964.

A personal memory of the line by one of the authors was travelling from Newcastle to Kelso for a school camp in 1954. We changed trains at Tweedmouth and research shows that, at that time, three trains a day from Newcastle stopped at Tweedmouth to connect with the train to Kelso; in this case a class G5 0-4-4T and two coaches.

BERWICK & KELSO BRANCH.—York, Newcastle, and Berwick.

Sprouston (Kelso) to Tweedmouth, at 1¼ morn.; 2¾ and 6 20 aft. On Sundays at 9 morn. and 7 aft.
Tweedmouth to Sprouston (for Kelso), at 7 morn., and 1½ and 8¾ aft. On Sundays at 7½ morn. and 5½ aft.
Fares.—Between Sprouston and Tweedmouth, 1st class, 4s.; 2nd class, 3s. 6d.; 3rd class, 2s. 4d.; gov., 1s. 9d.

This 1850 timetable was issued by the York, Newcastle & Berwick Railway.

The North Eastern passenger services as they were found in the 1895 timetable.

BERWICK, TWEEDMOUTH, and KELSO.—North Eastern.

Down.	mrn	mrn		mrn	mrn	aft	aft	aft		mrn	aft	Up.	mrn	mrn	aft	aft	aft	aft		mrn	aft
Berwick ..dep.	6 0	8 10		8 35	11 30	2 10	5 30	7 25		7 30	5 30	Kelso.......dep.	8 5	10 0	12 40	3 20	7 45	....		9 15	7 45
Tweedmouth..	6 10	8 20		8 45	11 40	2 20	5 30	7 35		7 40	5 40	Sprouston	8 10	10 5	12 45	3 25	7 50	....		9 20	7 50
Velvet Hall..	6 18	8 28		8 53	11 48	2 28	5 38	7 43		7 48	5 48	Carham........	8 16	10 10	12 50	3 30	7 55	....		9 25	7 55
Norham	6 24	8 34		8 59	11 54	2 34	5 44	7 49		7 54	5 54	Sunnilaws......	8 21	10 16	12 55	3 36	8 1	....		9 31	8 1
Twizel......	6 30	8 40		9 5	12 0	2 40	5 50	7 55		8 0	6 0	Coldstream....	8 28	10 23	1 3	3 43	8 8	8 34		9 38	8 8
Coldstream..	6 37	8 49		9 13	12 8	2 48	5 59	8 3		8 8	8 8	Twizel......	8 35	10 30	1 10	3 50	8 15	8 41		9 45	8 15
Sunnilaws......	....	....		9 20	12 14	2 54	6 6	8 9		8 15	6 15	Norham	8 42	10 37	1 16	3 57	8 22	8 48		9 52	8 22
Carham......	....	....		9 25	12 20	3 0	6 11	8 15		8 20	6 20	Velvet Hall....	8 49	10 44	1 23	4 4	8 39	8 55		9 59	8 29
Sprouston......	....	....		9 30	12 25	3 5	6 16	8 20		8 25	6 25	Tweedmuth 420	8 56	10 51	1 30	4 11	8 36	9 2		10 6	8 36
Kelso 524, 525 ar	....	....		9 35	12 30	3 10	6 21	8 25		8 30	6 30	Berwick 522 ar	9 5	11 0	1 40	4 20	8 45	9 10		10 15	8 45

BERWICK

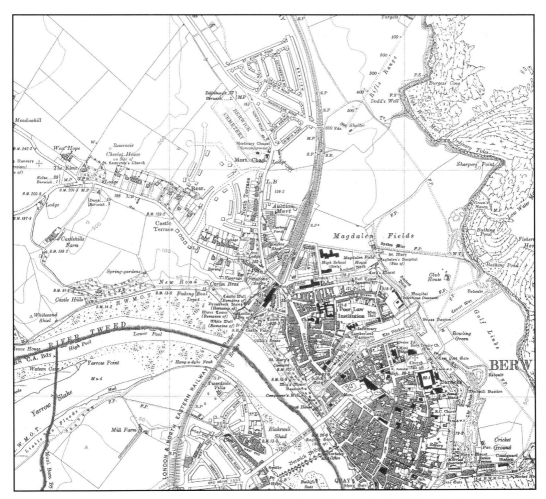

II. The Border town of Berwick was connected to the rail network in 1846 with the opening of the North British Railway line from Edinburgh Waverley. In 1850 it became part of the East Coast Main Line with the opening of the Royal Border Bridge connecting it to the York, Newcastle & Berwick Railway. Two routes, either side of the River Tweed linked it to St. Boswells on the Waverley Route, the line via Kelso opened in 1851 whilst the line via Duns opened in 1862. The station was rebuilt by the LNER in 1927 and was renamed Berwick-upon-Tweed on 1st January 1955. The 1961 census, the last before closure of the Kelso line, shows the population as 12,570. This 1932 map is at 6 inches to 1 mile.

For further views of Berwick see our _St. Boswells to Berwick via Duns_ and _Berwick to Drem_ albums.

Berwick is viewed from across the River Tweed on 25th June 2013. The lower 17th century road bridge on the left was replaced by the newer one in 1928 which, until the building of the by-pass in the 1980s, carried the A1 road. The old bridge today is part of a one way system and only carries traffic from Berwick into Tweedmouth. In the foreground is a wooden tidal jetty. (D.A.Lovett)

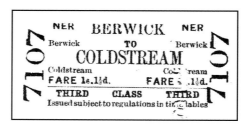

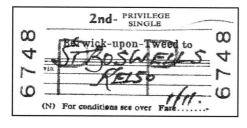

1.　　The 1927 station buildings and car park were viewed 'over the wall' from Railway Street on 24th July 1978. The original station was in a mock castle style, a small apology for laying the railway straight through the ruins of Berwick Castle. (A.Price/Colour Rail)

2.　　A3 class 4-6-2 no. 60096 *Papyrus* leaves with the 16.00 Glasgow to Leeds on 6th September 1955. The twin towers enclose the goods hoists for taking parcels traffic to and from the island platform. (H.C.Casserley)

3.   A3 class 4-6-2 no. 60096 *Papyrus* heads on to the Royal Border Bridge with the 16.00 Glasgow to Leeds on 6th September 1955. This is the same train as in picture no. 2. (H.C.Casserley)

4.   V2 class 2-6-2 no. 60926 enters the station on 13th August 1960. The photographer was at the southern end of the island platform which shows how close the station is to the bridge. The locomotive was allocated to Tweedmouth from where it was withdrawn on 1st August 1962. (N.E.Stead coll.)

5.   Deltic Class 55 Co-Co DE no. 9001 *St. Paddy* awaits departure from Berwick with a northbound express in August 1962. The bridge carried the A1 road before the bypass was built. (G.C.Bett/Transport Treasury)

6.   In marked contrast to the expresses running between London and Edinburgh, BR Standard 2MT 2-6-0 no. 78046 enters the station with a train from Kelso on 3rd July 1959. (Colour-Rail.com)

7.   HST power car no. 254010 pulls into Berwick with a train from Edinburgh on 7th March 1980. Electrification of the East Coast Main Line was authorised in 1984. The power was switched on in the Borders in March 1991 with the first electric train running on 12th June 1991 and regular services from 8th July 1991. (Rail Photoprints)

8.   The station was refurbished in 2009 with new lifts, glass canopies on the island platform, and improved facilities for passengers. This is the view looking north on 24th June 2013. (D.A.Lovett)

SOUTH OF
BERWICK

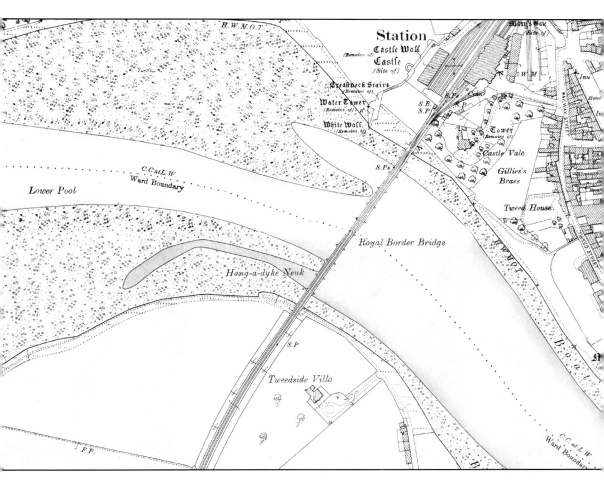

III.   The Royal Border Bridge seen on the 1909 edition. The River Tweed was at various times in British history the border between England and Scotland. Berwick was a Scottish Borough until 1482 when it became part of England. Although the border has been 2½ miles north of Berwick since the union in 1707, the bridge over the River Tweed linking Berwick on the north bank and Tweedmouth on the south has always been known as the Royal Border Bridge. The imposing stone structure comprises 28 arches each spanning 60ft and is 2162ft in length. The line is 121ft above sea level and gives excellent views of the mouth of the River and Berwick itself. The opening of the Royal Border Bridge on 29th August 1850, enabled the North British Railway route from Edinburgh to link with the York, Newcastle & Berwick line which had terminated at Tweedmouth since 1847.

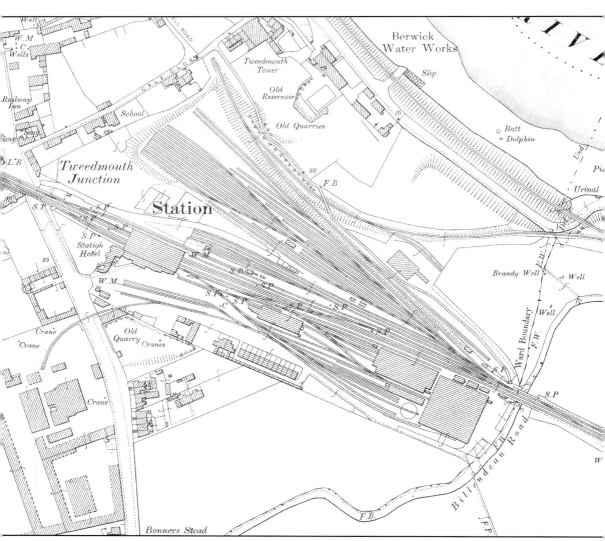

IV.   The survey is from 1909. The harbour branch to Tweed Dock was opened in 1878 and comprised a zigzag route to gain height (top right). It will be covered in a future album. The station had an overall roof but this had gone before 1930. Tweedmouth station was originally the terminus of the line from Newcastle which opened on 29th March 1847. The imposing station increased in importance with the opening of the branch to Sprouston on 27th July 1849 but lost most of that when the bridge was completed in 1850. The station closed with the Kelso line on 15th June 1964. A small yard remains but all traces of the station have long since vanished.

9.　　Gresley designed 4-6-2 A3 class no. 2746 *Fairway* enters Tweedmouth with a southbound train in the 1930s. (G.C.Bett/Transport Treasury)

10.　　A view of Tweedmouth is from the train as A2 Class 4-6-2 no. 60509 *Waverley* heads south on 10th August 1949 over the Royal Border Bridge. (A.G.Forsyth/Initial Photographics)

11.   A4 class 4-6-2 no. 60009 *Union of South Africa* heads north with a train of Pullman cars in June 1959. (Colour-Rail.com)

12.   J39 class 0-6-0 no. 64925 hauls a single coach towards Tweedmouth, whilst K3 class 2-6-0 no. 61876 heads north with a goods train. Both are crossing the Royal Border Bridge on 3rd July 1959. (K.Fairey/Colour-Rail.com)

13.　　The station is viewed from the road with the main entrance to the platforms situated underneath the arches. It was photographed on 14th April 1963. (H.C.Casserley)

14.　　This is a view about 1960 of the Down platform with the locomotive depot in the distance, on the left of the platform canopy. Included in the buildings was the Station Hotel. (North Eastern Railway Association)

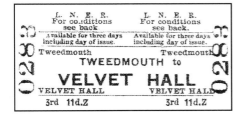
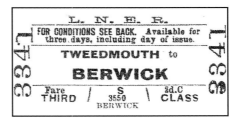

15.   Class D30/2 4-4-0 no. 62424 *Claverhouse* was allocated to St. Margarets (Edinburgh) until its withdrawal on 31st August 1957. Here it is marshalling empty stock for a return excursion to Peebles from Spittal beach (Tweedmouth). (C.J.B.Sanderson/N.E.Stead coll.)

16.   BR standard 2MT 2-6-0 no. 78049 pauses at Tweedmouth with a train for Kelso on 15th August 1961. At Tweedmouth the branch train had to reverse in either direction and only the down platform was used. Trains from Kelso entered the station on the down platform and the engine ran around the train to haul it to Berwick. Trains from Berwick ran through the station on the up line to a point level with the engine shed and then pushed its train into the down platform. It then ran around its train and proceeded north onto the branch. This procedure was required as the only lockable points were south of the station. (H.Forsyth/Colour-Rail.com)

17.   An express hauled by Class A2 4-6-2 no. 60519 *Honeyway* passes a local train with 2-6-0 no. 78049 which has called at Tweedmouth on 8th September 1962 (B.Johnson/A.E.Young coll.)

18.   The station is viewed from the engine shed area on 3rd September 1962. (K.L.Taylor/A.E.Young coll.)

19.   A3 Class 4-6-2 no. 60075 *St. Frusquin* calls with a southbound train on 4th July 1959. The photograph is enhanced by a NER shunting signal. (N.E.Stead coll.)

20.   We are looking south to the shed area. In front of the signal box is V2 Class 2-6-2 no. 60822 from Dundee, and a line of K3 2-6-0s awaiting scrap in 1962. (N.E.Stead coll.)

TWEEDMOUTH ENGINE SHED

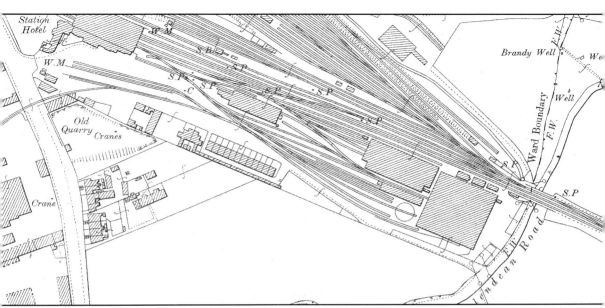

V.   Tweedmouth Engine Shed is shown in 1909 when it serviced only North Eastern locomotives and was located south of the station to the west of the East Coast Main Line. Some three months after the line from Newcastle was completed, an engine shed was provided at Tweedmouth opening on 1st July 1847. After closure of the North British shed at Berwick by the LNER in 1924 all locomotive activity was concentrated at Tweedmouth. In BR days the shed code was 52D. It closed on 19th June 1966 and the four track straight shed was subsequently demolished. The round house remains in industrial use as part of a builders merchants although it did suffer severe fire damage on 14th January 2010.

21.   On 18th September 1955 Tweedmouth had on shed from left to right class V2 no. 60835, class K3s nos 61875, 61917, 61952 and class V2 no. 60801 in 1955. (G.W.Morrison)

22. Inside Tweedmouth shed on 18th September 1955 was, from left to right, J39 nos. 64917, 64925, J25 class no. 65720, J21 class no. 65091, J25 class no. 65662 and J21 no. 65099. (G.W.Morrison)

23. On the 6th June 1959, the London, Brighton & South Coast Railway A1X Class 0-6-0T no. 82 *Boxhill* is seen in store a long way from home. This locomotive with 4-4-0 no. 1737 and 4-4-0 no. 563 arrived at the shed in July 1958 and stayed until July 1959. They are now in the National Railway Museum Collection. Two J39 class locomotives are beyond the turntable. (A.Snapper/B. McCartney coll.)

24. The rear of the former round house building was still standing on 12th September 2010 when viewed from the road. It has since been damaged by fire. (D.A.Lovett)

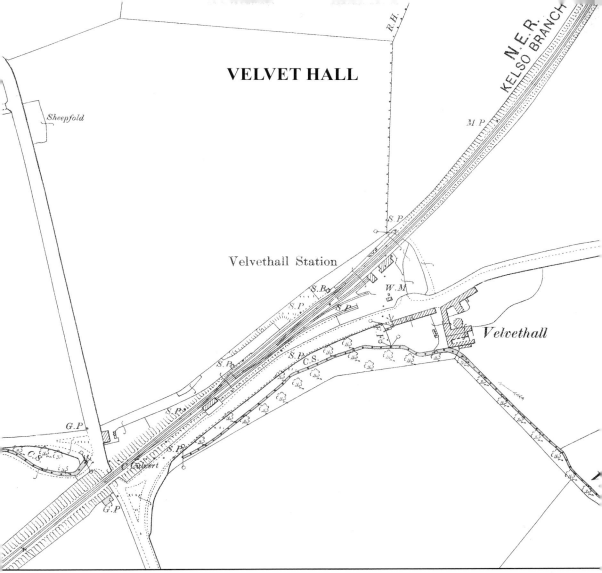

VELVET HALL

Sheepfold

Velvethall Station

Velvethall

N.E.R. KELSO BRANCH

VI. This is the 1903 edition. Velvet Hall opened on 27th July 1849 and closed on 4th July 1955, nine years before the line's passenger services were withdrawn. Goods traffic continued until 29th March 1965. The station building was subsequently converted for residential use.

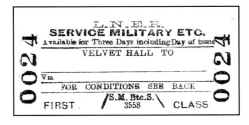

25.   This is a 1925 view as the station building has been extended on the left. The large building on the right is a covered coal and lime store. The photographer is facing towards Berwick. (J.Alsop coll.)

26.   There seems no danger of a train arriving during the time this undated photograph was taken. (A.E.Young coll.)

27.   BR Standard 2MT No. 78046, a Hawick engine, pauses at Velvet Hall with a local service in 1960. The goods shed is shown more clearly. There was another goods shed further south within the goods sidings. (Milepost 92½)

28.   Velvet Hall station is seen here on 24th June 2013 and is now a private house. The platforms were behind the building which was viewed from the road,. (D.A.Lovett)

NORHAM

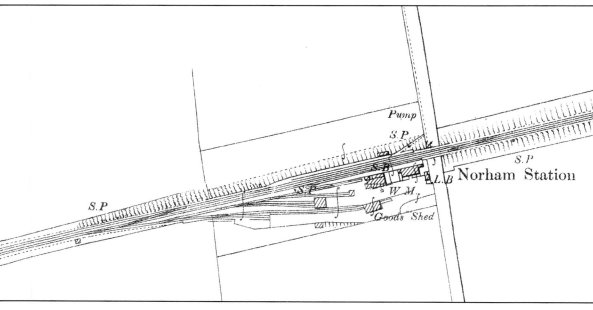

VII. The 1906 survey is shown at 20ins to 1 mile.

    Norham opened with the line on 27th July 1849 and closed with it when passenger services were withdrawn on 15th June 1964. Goods services ceased on 29th March 1965. The station was superbly preserved by its last Station Master Peter Short who turned it into a museum as well as running his coal merchant's business from it. Norham Castle was built in 1121 and featured in wars between England and Scotland. After 1596 it fell into ruin and is now owned by English Heritage. It was painted by Turner and here photographed on 24th June 2013. (D.A.Lovett)

29. This is a classic view of the station, looking towards Kelso and taken on the 14th July 1952. The original signal box was on the platform at the end of the station building and was replaced by the present one.(A.G.Ellis/ARPT)

30. This is a view taken on 2nd May 1952. The signal box nameboard had been blacked out in World War 2 to fox any potential spies. The goods yard on the south side of the station had four short sidings. The shed is a double covered coal and lime store. (C.J.B.Sanderson/ ARPT/R.W.Lynn coll.)

31. V3 class 2-6-2T no. 67606 calls with a west bound train for Kelso. This locomotive was shedded at Hawick from 1956 to 1959 to work this line from its subshed at St. Boswells. It was withdrawn in December 1962. (R.W.Lynn coll.)

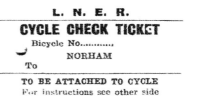

32. The preserved signal box in the late 1970's complete with diagram and block instruments looks ready to accept its next train. Norham was preserved by Station Master Peter Short, but the museum was closed on the death of his wife in September 2013 and the station was put up for sale. (R.B.McCartney)

The 1960 timetable after closure of several stations that occurred in 1955

Table 24 **ST. BOSWELLS and BERWICK-UPON-TWEED**

Miles	Week Days only		am	am A	am S	am E	pm A	pm B
—	**St. Boswells**	dep	**6 22**	**8 25**	**1124**	**11 30**	**4 0**	**7 15**
3	Maxton		..	8 31	..	..	4 6	7 20
5½	Rutherford		..	8 36	1134	11 40	4 11	7 25
8½	Roxburgh		..	8 43	1140	11 46	4 18	7 30
11½	Kelso	arr	6 43	8 48	1145	11 51	4 23	7 35
		dep	..	8 50	..	..	4 40	..
21½	Coldstream		..	9 9	..	..	5 4	..
27¾	Norham		..	9 19	..	..	5 14	..
33¾	Tweedmouth		..	9F37	..	..	5F32	..
35	**Berwick-upon-Tweed**	arr	..	**9 40**	..	..	**5 35**	..
90½	Newcastle	arr	..	1T24	..	..	7D45	..

Miles	Week Days only		am	am A	am S	pm E	pm C	pm A
	Newcastle	dep	..	6 55	..	..	..	4G30
—	**Berwick-upon-Tweed**	dep	..	**9 56**	..	..	..	**6 37**
1¼	Tweedmouth		..	10F 6	..	..	..	6F47
7¼	Norham		..	10 17	..	..	..	6 58
13½	Coldstream		..	10 27	..	..	..	7 11
23½	Kelso	arr	..	10 43	..	..	..	7 28
		dep	7 35	10 45	1152	2 21	7 40	7 50
26½	Roxburgh		7 42	10 52	1159	2 29	..	7 57
29½	Rutherford		7 49	10 58	12 5	2 35	..	8 6
32	Maxton		7 54	..	1210	2 40	..	8 11
35	**St. Boswells**	arr	**8 1**	**11 8**	**1216**	**2 46**	**7 58**	**8 17**

A Through Train between St. Boswells and Berwick-upon-Tweed
B Through Diesel Train from Edinburgh dep 5 5 pm
C Through Diesel Train to Edinburgh arr 9 1 pm
D Arr Newcastle 7 32 pm on Fridays until 26th August and on Saturdays from 25th June
E Except Saturdays
F Arr 7 minutes *earlier*
G Connection at Tweedmouth. On Saturdays dep Newcastle 4 45 pm
p pm
S Saturdays only
T On Saturdays arr Newcastle 12 50 pm

Sprouston, Carham, Sunilaws, Twizell and Velvet Hall served by road services operated by Scottish Omnibuses Ltd.

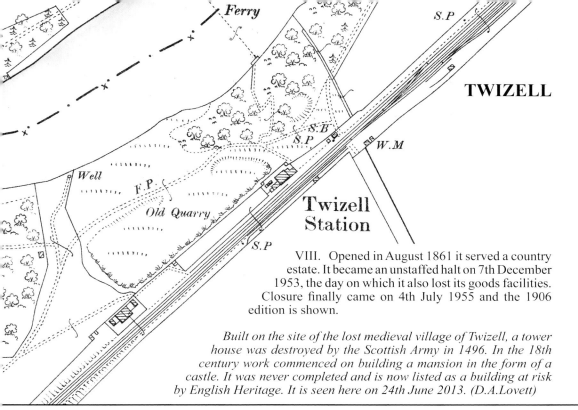

TWIZELL

Twizell
Station

VIII. Opened in August 1861 it served a country estate. It became an unstaffed halt on 7th December 1953, the day on which it also lost its goods facilities. Closure finally came on 4th July 1955 and the 1906 edition is shown.

Built on the site of the lost medieval village of Twizell, a tower house was destroyed by the Scottish Army in 1496. In the 18th century work commenced on building a mansion in the form of a castle. It was never completed and is now listed as a building at risk by English Heritage. It is seen here on 24th June 2013. (D.A.Lovett)

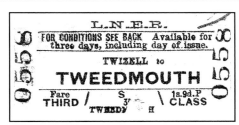

33.   This is an undated photograph looking towards Kelso. The main station building is on the right with the raised platform beyond it. In the distance are two semi detached railway cottages. (A.E. Young coll.)

34.   25th April 1952, the station had a rather neglected air. The signal box covers the station and the two goods sidings to the north east. There was no goods shed. The porter is making heavy weather carrying his parcel. (ARPT)

35.　　The former station master's house remains whilst the trackbed runs left to right across the front and was a gravel roadway when visited on 16th September 2013. (D.A.Lovett)

TWIZELL VIADUCT

36.　　Just beyond Twizell station, the line crossed the River Till on a large curved viaduct. The Kelso bound train is being hauled by a class B1 4-6-0, most probably no. 61357 one of four locos of the 1350 series with a riveted tender. (C.J.B.Sanderson/R.W.Lynn coll.)

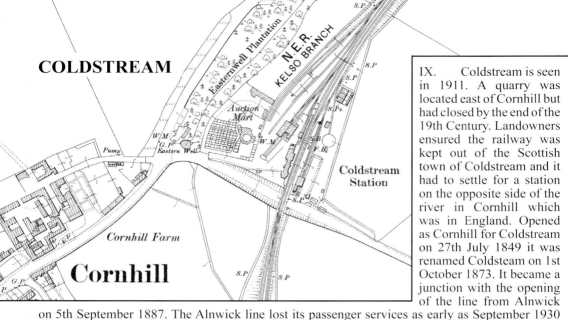

COLDSTREAM

Auction Mart

Coldstream Station

Cornhill Farm

Cornhill

IX. Coldstream is seen in 1911. A quarry was located east of Cornhill but had closed by the end of the 19th Century. Landowners ensured the railway was kept out of the Scottish town of Coldstream and it had to settle for a station on the opposite side of the river in Cornhill which was in England. Opened as Cornhill for Coldstream on 27th July 1849 it was renamed Coldsteam on 1st October 1873. It became a junction with the opening of the line from Alnwick on 5th September 1887. The Alnwick line lost its passenger services as early as September 1930 although it remained open for goods traffic to serve Wooler until 29th July 1965 when Coldstream also closed to goods traffic. Coldstream lost its passenger services on 15th June 1964. The population of Coldstream was 1287 in 1961.

X. The line for Kelso heads to the west whilst the line to the south served Alnwick, as seen in this 1898 map. South of Cornhill, sidings were provided at Campfield in the 19th Century to serve military camps. They were close to the junction with the Wooler line, the arrival of which probably resulted in their removal. Campfield is marked at the bottom of the map below.

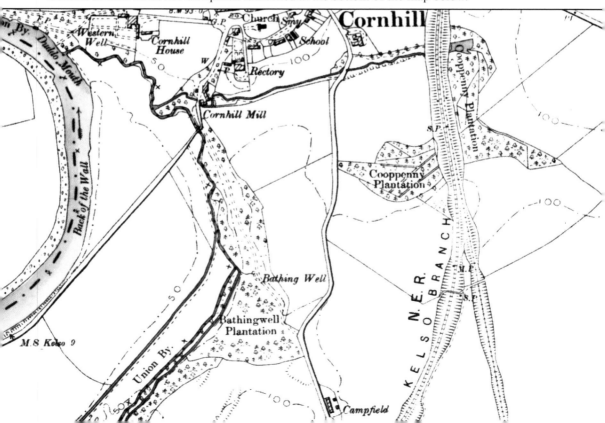

Here is the River Tweed at Coldstream from the Scottish side of the river on 24th June 2013 with the town in the background. The statue is of Charles Marjoribanks, the Liberal MP for Berwickshire from 1832 until his death the following year at the age of 39. (D.A.Lovett)

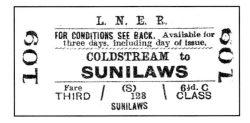

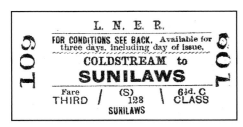

Extract from Bradshaw's Guide for 1866.
(Reprinted by Middleton Press 2011)

CORNHILL (for Coldstream).

Telegraph station at Tweedmouth, 12¼ miles.

HOTEL.—Railway.

FAIR.—December 6th.

Close at hand is Flodden Field, noted for the battle fought between James IV. of Scotland and the Earl of Surrey, in 1513, in which the former was defeated and slain. Near the church is a mineral spring, and traces of a castle taken by the Scots in 1549.

COLDSTREAM stands opposite an old ford of the river, and being on Scottish ground, it has become, like Gretna Green, a place for runaway matches—Lord.Brougham's, for instance. Here Monk waited his time to declare for Charles II., with some veterans who formed the earliest regiment of the Coldstream Guards. *Lees*, seat of Sir J. Marjoribanks, Bart.

37. The station staff have lined up for the cameraman who was there in about 1910. Both the station and the station house are fine stone buildings. (J.Alsop coll.)

38. Class D1 4-4-0 no. 62208 is on a St. Boswells train. These Great Northern engines were declared surplus with some transferred to Scotland as early as 1925. They were extremely unpopular in Scotland, known as 'Ponies' and regarded as cast offs. This locomotive was withdrawn from Hawick on 31st July 1950. (R.W.Lynn coll.)

39. This fine overall view of the station was taken in March 1955. We are facing towards Berwick and the goods shed is on the left, behind the station and signal box. The Auction Mart was beyond that. There was not an engine shed but a turntable was behind the buildings on the right. (R.W.Lynn coll.)

40. A permanent way trolley pauses on the turntable in 1961. This gives a good view of the signal box and the goods shed behind it.
(R.Oakley/
Colour-Rail.com)

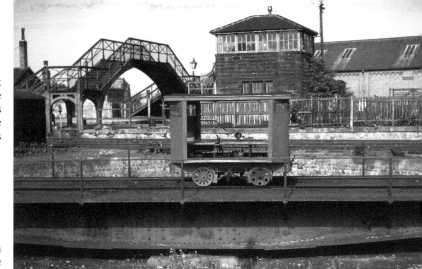

41 Coldstream station building is seen from the approach road on 14th April 1963. The Auction Mart is behind us.(R.M.Casserley)

42. The station is under siege during the visit of class B1 4-6-0 no. 61324 during the SLS/BLS Railtour no.2 on 14th April 1963. The B1 is 'wrong line', reversing on to the train which has returned from Wooler hauled by 2-6-0 no. 46474.
(R.M.Casserley)

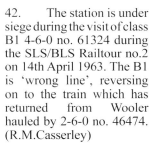

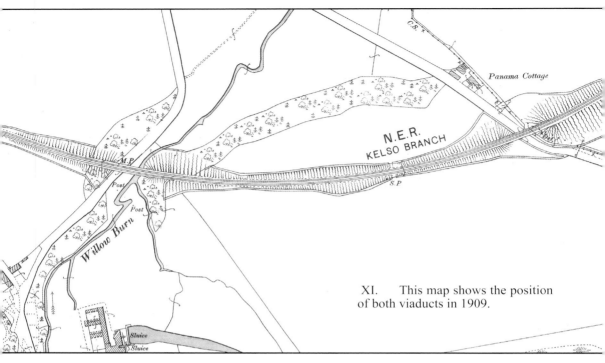

XI.   This map shows the position
of both viaducts in 1909.

43.   West Learmouth viaduct remains in place and is seen here on 18th August 2001.
(A.E.Young)

LEARMOUTH SIDING

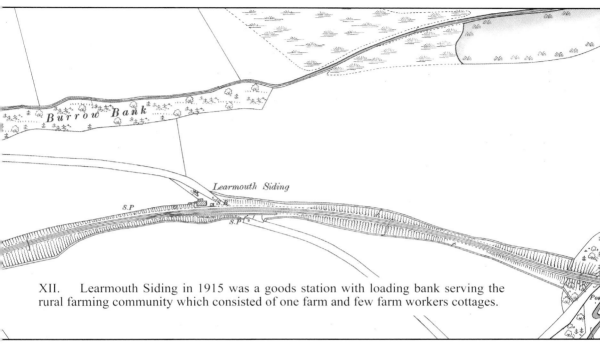

XII.   Learmouth Siding in 1915 was a goods station with loading bank serving the rural farming community which consisted of one farm and few farm workers cottages.

44.   The simple signal cabin seen here is the SB on map XII, controlling Learmouth Siding. It was recorded at the time of closure. The insert shows the remains of the loading bank and siding on 16th September 2013. (J.E.Hay)

SUNILAWS

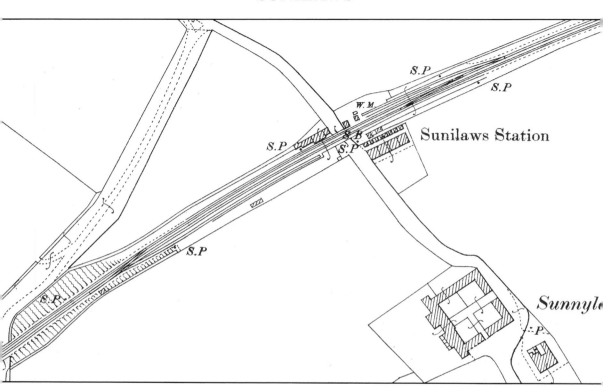

XIII.   The 1909 edition is at 40ins to 1 mile. Opened as Wark in July 1859 it was renamed Sunilaws on 1st October 1871. The North British Railway already had a station at Wark on the Border Counties line (see our Hexham to Hawick album) which had opened in 1859, so renaming was carried out to avoid confusion for both passengers and staff. The village of Wark on the bank of the River Tweed was a mile away. Sunilaws, sometimes spelt Sunnylaws, was named after a nearby farm. Its rural location ensured its early closure to passenger traffic on 4th July 1955 whilst goods traffic remained until 25th January 1965. The station site is easily identified, the station building is in residential use and the down platform and a loading bank still in place.

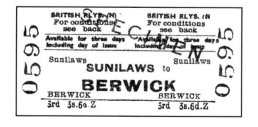

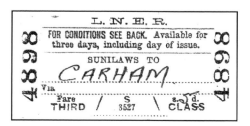

45.   A fine view of the station shows the staggered platform height on the left and the loading bank on the right. The photographer was facing towards Tweedmouth. (R.W.Lynn coll.)

46.   The line curved towards Kelso with the level crossing for the road to Sunnylaws Farm. Behind the signal box was a set of cottages. The station and station platform were on the right. (A.E.Young coll.)

47.   Accidents do happen, the remnants of the level crossing gates are evident after a train went through them when running early. The crossing keeper was distraught. (I.Pringle)

48.   Looking towards Berwick in 2013, the down platform had recently had the farm cottages behind it refurbished and extended. The circles highlight two small sections of rail protruding from the tarmac that once crossed the minor road which linked it with the nearby village of Wark. (D.A.Lovett)

EAST OF CARHAM

49.　　This was the boundary marker between the North Eastern and Scottish regions of British Railways near Carham, Northumberland, photographed in April 1967. (R.B.McCartney)

50.　　J39 class 0-6-0 no. 64941 crossing the Border at Carham with a Tweedmouth to St Boswells service on 14th May 1955. Built in 1938 the locomotive was allocated to Tweedmouth shed from where it was withdrawn on 3rd December 1962. (C.J.B.Sanderson/ARPT)

CARHAM

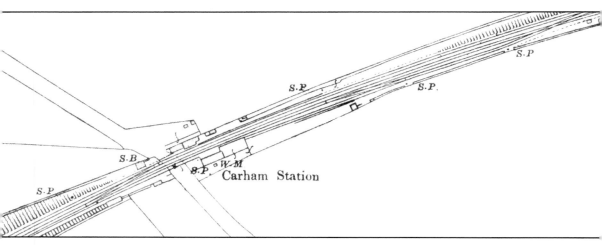

Carham Station

XIV.   Here is the edition of 1921. The English village of Carham was in a unique position of having its railway station in Scotland. Carham opened on 27 July 1849 and closed on 4th July 1955. Goods traffic survived until 18th May 1964. Due south of the village was the Skiddaw Tile Company which had sidings located on the north side of the line. There was also a lime kiln to the east of Carham with a rail connection to the north.

This is the centre of Carham on 24th June 2013. (D.A.Lovett)

51.　　The platforms were staggered either side of the level crossing with the main buildings on the Tweedmouth side. This view is looking towards Kelso. (North Eastern Railway Association)

52.　　This panorama is in the opposite direction showing the signal box and the waiting room on the down side. (ARPT)

SPROUSTON

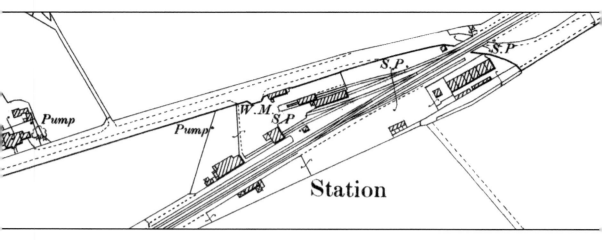

XV.   This edition is from 1898. This was originally the terminus of the line from Tweedmouth and opened with the line on 27th July 1849. As a result it had generous facilities including an engine shed. The line was later extended towards Kelso to form a connection with the NBR line from St. Boswells. Although the station closed to passengers on 4th July 1955, it remained open for goods traffic and became an unstaffed public siding on 15th June 1964 before closing completely on 25th January 1965. The station building remains in residential use having been extended since closure.

The pleasant village green is seen on 24th June 2013 with the church or Kirk which dates from 1781. The road to the right led to the former station. (D.A.Lovett)

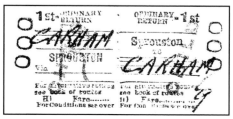

53.   An overall view of the station is looking east on 14th March 1955. (C.J.B.Sanderson/ARPT)

54.   A close up of the station buildings was shot from a passing train enroute to Kelso. Behind the signal is the water tower and engine shed. (N.E.Stead coll.)

55. An unidentified BR standard 2MT class 2-6-0 is shunting the yard with the daily freight as it passes the former single road engine shed. (A.E.Young coll.)

56. This is the platform side of the extended station building as seen on 18th August 2001 with part of the platform and track bed forming part of the garden. (A.E.Young)

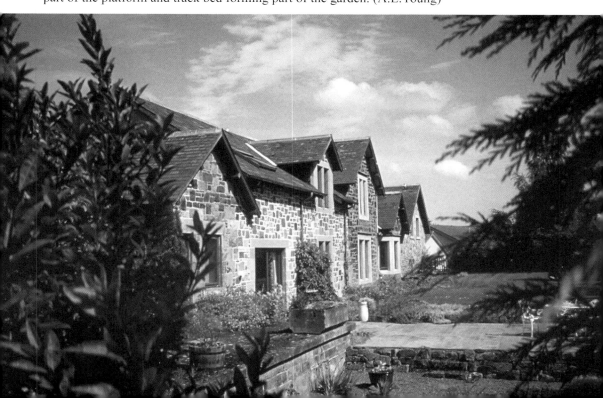

SPROUSTON
LOCO SHED

57.   Sprouston engine shed was photographed on 31st August 1959. The first shed opened in 1863 and was destroyed in a gale on 14th October 1881. A brick replacement opened the following year and was officially closed in 1916. It stood until closure of the line in the mid-1960s and was then demolished. (R.S.Carpenter)

58.   During World War II the shed was used to store GWR City Class 4-4-0 no. 3440 *City of Truro* which was evacuated from the then York Railway Museum. This rare picture shows the historic locomotive with protective covering being shunted out of the shed.
(R.W.Lynn coll.)

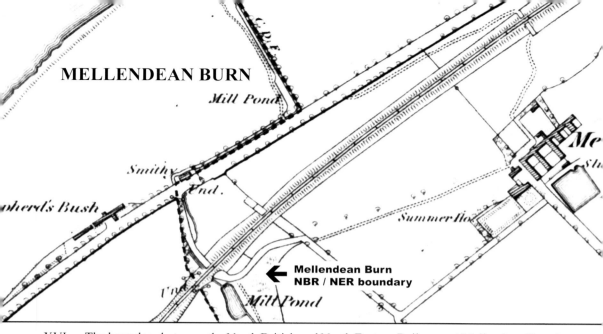

MELLENDEAN BURN

Mill Pond

Smithy
End.

herd's Bush

Summer fle

Me

Sh

Mill Pond

Mellendean Burn
NBR / NER boundary

XVI.   The boundary between the North British and North Eastern Railways at Mellendean Burn is indicated on this 1898 map. Quite why they went to such efforts to form a physical link is a mystery as they operated as two separate branch lines each terminating in the same station in Kelso. As late as 1967 at Mellendean there was also a noticeable change between the NER ash ballast and the NBR stone ballast. The through route only reached its potential when flooding closed many lines in the Borders in 1948.

KELSO

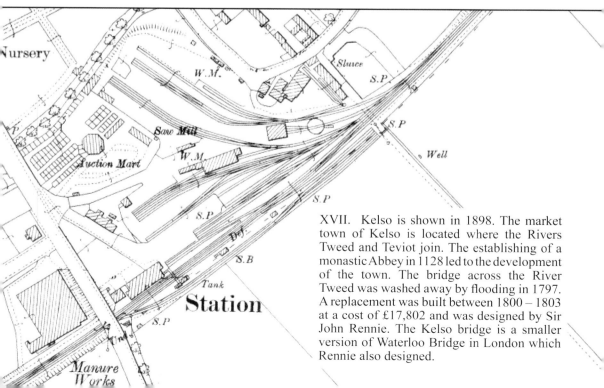

Nursery

W.M.

Sluice

S.P.

S.P

Saw Mill

W.M.

Well

Auction Mart

S.P.

S.P.

Def.

S.B

Tank

Station

S.P.

Manure
Works

XVII.   Kelso is shown in 1898. The market town of Kelso is located where the Rivers Tweed and Teviot join. The establishing of a monastic Abbey in 1128 led to the development of the town. The bridge across the River Tweed was washed away by flooding in 1797. A replacement was built between 1800 – 1803 at a cost of £17,802 and was designed by Sir John Rennie. The Kelso bridge is a smaller version of Waterloo Bridge in London which Rennie also designed.

The cobbled square in Kelso is seen here on 24th June 2013. It is unique in Scotland in being served by four cobbled streets. Kelso Town Hall forms the centrepiece. (D.A.Lovett)

59.   The arrival of the railway was not without difficulty. The Duke of Roxburghe ensured that the railway was kept out of the town and the local residents had to cross the river into Maxwellhaugh, where Kelso station was built. These difficulties delayed the arrival of both the North Eastern and North British lines which did not reach the town until 27th January 1851. Kelso became an uneasy station with both the NER and NBR refusing to co-operate in providing a through service. It closed on 15th June 1964 although goods trains continued until 30th March 1968. The 1961 census shows it had a population of 4,206 around the time of closure. Kelso today has a population of some 6,000. Kelso station is seen in about 1909. The locomotive is 0-4-2 no. 324, a Hurst engine built by Beyer Peacock. It was the Jedburgh branch engine and is putting a horsebox on to the rear of the NER Berwick train.(J.Alsop coll.)

60.   Class G9 0-4-4T no. 9353 is on a branch train at Kelso. The locomotive was shedded at Hawick for the Kelso and Jedburgh branches. The G class (Reid class M) were the last 0-4-4T's built by the NBR with the 12 locos appearing in 1909. This locomotive was withdrawn in October 1937 and the class went by 1940.(A.G.Ellis/ARPT)

61.   This photograph has us looking towards St. Boswells as it was in the 1930s with the main station building on the up platform. The up platform was extended under the road bridge alongside the agricultural chemicals factory. (LOSA)

62. This is another 1930s view. The signal box was located on the down platform which was an island platform. The photograph was taken under the footbridge and on the right is the water tank with a large poster. (LOSA)

63. Reid designed Class C15 4-4-2T no. 9265 was built in July 1913 by the Yorkshire Engine Company. It was allocated to Hawick as no. 67472 on nationalisation, but was withdrawn from Polmont in April 1956. (R.W.Lynn coll.)

64. Class A3 4-6-2 no. 100 *Spearmint* was renumbered from 2796 in July 1946 and to no. 60100 in April 1949. so this diversion through Kelso of the Pullman train 'Queen of Scots' was most likely to have been as a result of the August 1948 floods. (R.W.Lynn coll.)

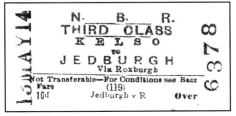

65.   Kelso was busy in this 1960s north easterly view. The Class 100 DMU's destination blind reads Edinburgh which probably makes it the 7.40pm departure. The hooped tablet is on the driver's desk. This left Edinburgh at 5.05pm, all stations via Peebles, to arrive at Kelso at 7.35pm. It will return via the Waverley Route stopping only at Galashiels, Eskbank & Dalkeith, and Portobello. Class 2MT 2-6-0 78046 will then follow with its train as far as St. Boswells. (R.B.McCartney coll.)

66.   This is the view of the engine shed and goods yard from near the grain silos. In the distance is the Auction Mart. The Kelso shed was the same style as those at Duns and St. Boswells. (N.E.Stead coll.)

67.   Class Y1 4WVBT no. 68138 was shunting the goods shed. This Sentinel locomotive was their no. 7134 and was taken into stock in 1927. As LNER no. 9529 it was the only Sentinel locomotive in the Scottish area and from 1928 to 1955 it spent its life in Kelso. In August of that year it went to Ayr to replace LMS Sentinel no. 47182. It stayed there until withdrawal in January 1959. (N.E.Stead coll.)

68.   Class 08 0-6-0 Diesel Shunter no. D3891 collects wagons from in front of the large goods shed for the last time on 29th March 1968. (Inset) Ian Fergusson shines the headboard he made for the last freight to Kelso which was attached to D3891 (R.B.McCartney)

69.   The bridge over the station has now gone and a new by-pass built on the former rail alignment. Only the former agricultural chemicals factory, which once adjoined the extended up platform, gives any indication that the railway even existed here. It was photographed on 24th June 2013.(D.A.Lovett)

Solitary, stark closure pronouncement pasted to the British Railways notice board at Kelso in March 1968 (R.B.McCartney)

Extract from Bradshaw's Guide for 1866. (Reprinted by Middleton Press 2011)

KELSO.

A telegraph station.

HOTELS.—Cross Keys, and Queen's Head.

MARKET DAY.—Friday.

RACES in spring and autumn.

FAIRS.—Monthly, and second Friday in May, 6th July, August, and 2nd November.

KELSO is a market town (population about 4,783) in Scotland, which stands on the north side of the Tweed, opposite the junction of that river with the Teviot. It may be considered as the provincial capital of the surrounding fertile country, and noted for its manufacture of woollen tweeds, &c. Its inhabitants are polished, well-informed, and live in a style of considerable elegance, or rather luxury. The situation of the town is uncommonly beautiful It stands on the bank of a noble river, at the foot of that fertile tract of country which descends gradually from the heights of Lammermuir, and terminates on the borders of the Tweed. Here Scott's *Border Minstrelsy* was first published by Ballantyne, and in 1800 Rennie erected a noble five-arched bridge.

KELSO ENGINE SHED

Kelso engine shed opened in January 1851 and remained in use until July 1955.
Still standing 10 years later it was demolished after closure of the line in 1968.

70.   This official photograph marks the arrival at Kelso in September 1923 of NBR 'Petrol
Engine No. 1'. Costing £1,200, it was then fitted with a much larger cab at Cowlairs Works,
Glasgow, returning to Kelso in December 1927. It was classified by the LNER as Z6 class no. 8431.
In July 1930 it was transferred to Ware in the former Great Eastern area. In 1943 it was classified
at Y11 class. Its BR number at first was 68189 and then was no. 15099. It survived until November
1956. Its driver at Kelso was an ex-horse driver. It replaced several shunting horses, known locally
as 'Hairy Pilots'. (R.W.Lynn coll.)

71.   NBR G Class (LNER Y9) 0-4-0ST no. 9546 is on Kelso shed on 24th August 1927. The
locomotive was later renumbered 8122. A Y9 class locomotive came down from St. Margarets shed
to deputise for the usual Y1 no. 9529. (R.W.Lynn coll.)

72. D30 Class 4-4-0 no. 62435 *Norna* stands outside Kelso shed circa 1958-9. The shed had officially closed in July 1955, but was still used by visiting engines. (R.S.Carpenter)

WALLACE NICK

XVIII. Until the issues surrounding access into Kelso were settled, the North British line from St. Boswells was forced to terminate at Wallace Nick on 17th June 1850. It closed with extension into Maxwellhaugh where Kelso station was located on 27th July 1851. Services from Tweedmouth were extended into Kelso on the same date. The short lived terminus at Wallace Nick had disappeared by the time this 6ins to the mile map was surveyed in 1858 and published in 1863.

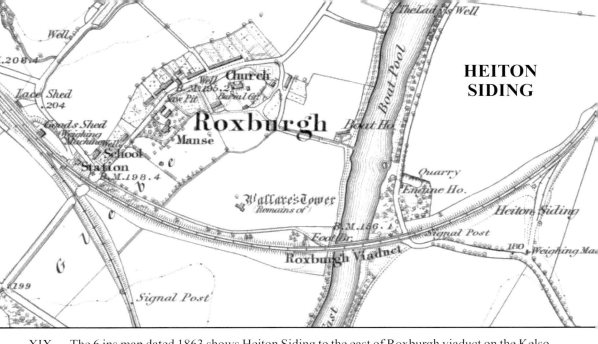

XIX.   The 6 ins map dated 1863 shows Heiton Siding to the east of Roxburgh viaduct on the Kelso line. The line from the station running south is the Jedburgh branch. A goods station consisting of two sidings was provided here from the opening of the line and in 1865 was the site of three derailments. The sidings were positioned here as there was no road crossing of the river to access the facilities at Roxburgh Junction. The last ever British Rail service to operate in the Borders during 1998/9 was not a train but a bus service for pupils who lived in Heiton and went to school in Roxburgh. See caption 75.

73.   BR Standard 2MT 2-6-0 no. 78048 is approaching Heiton with the 11.30 St. Boswells to Kelso on 30th May 1962. The photographer is unfortunately standing with Heiton Siding behind him - depriving us of that view. The siding closed to goods traffic on 23rd March 1964. (M.Mensing)

ROXBURGH VIADUCT

74.   Class J39 0-6-0 no. 64941 is crossing Roxburgh viaduct on its approach to Roxburgh station with a train to St. Boswells. Roxburgh viaduct has 13 arches, six of which span the River Teviot.. (C.J.B.Sanderson/ARPT)

75.   British Railways' last passenger service was a school bus between the villages of Heiton and Roxburgh which ran between August 1998 and March 1999. This arose because BR (Residuary) was renovating this viaduct. The viaduct has an iron footbridge attached to it, which had to be closed during the course of the work. This was opposed by locals, because children from Heiton used the bridge to walk to school in Roxburgh. Any alternative route was miles further via country roads with no pavements. BRB paid for the service which was arranged with the school and a local bus company. This is the view from the village on 25th June 2011. (A.E.Young)

ROXBURGH

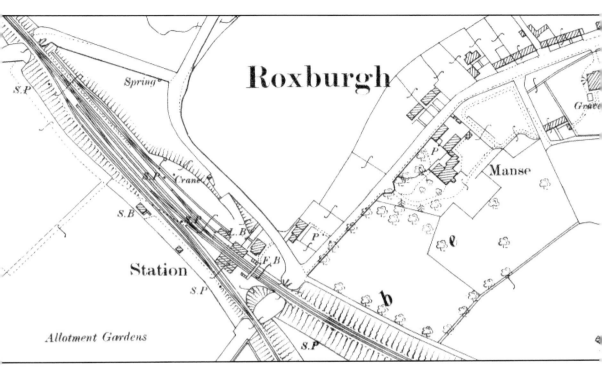

XX.   Roxburgh was once an important Royal Burgh whose castle and town were destroyed by the English in 1460. It lay some two miles north east of the present village. The original town gave its name to the county in which it stood, but after it was destroyed Jedburgh took over as the county town. The arrival of the railway saw a station opened on 17th June 1850. It was renamed Roxburgh Junction in 1856 to coincide with the opening of the Jedburgh branch but reverted to its original name around 1883. It closed to passengers on 15th June 1964 and closed to goods with the closure of the Jedburgh branch on 10th August 1964. The station house and the bridge abutments of both lines survive, the Jedburgh line is now a footpath. The map is from 1898

The village of Roxburgh is viewed on 24th June 2013. (D.A.Lovett)

76.   A 1890s view of the station buildings with Wheatley's standard 0-6-0 no. 295 posing with the staff. 70 of this class were built in batches with minor variations, from 1867 onwards. 37 lasted until LNER days but no. 295 was not one of them. The last was withdrawn in 1937. (J.Alsop coll.)

77.   A snow storm in December 1906 saw this Edinburgh to Kelso train stranded near Roxburgh. The event was captured by a postcard. The locomotive is no. 486, one of the 'Abbotsford' class of 4-4-0s as rebuilt in 1904 (D28). The Edinburgh to Kelso service worked via Peebles and Galashiels to Kelso and survived until the arrival of diesel multiple units. (R.Jack/J.Alsop coll.)

78.   The signal box stood at the rear of the down platform. A train heads towards St. Boswells in this 1930s view. (LOSA)

ROXBURGH (North British).

POPULATION, about 1,141.

A telegraph station.

This place was formerly the capital of the county. The moat of the castle still remains. Kings Alexander II. and III. were married here in great pomp. Close to a holly in the river, James II. was killed by the bursting of a cannon, in 1460. Good purple trout abound in the streams. In the vicinity are *Makerstoun*, the fine country seat of Sir T. Brisbane, Bart., and *Smailholm Tower*, "the scene of one of Scott's ballads, and the frequent resort of his grandfather."

Extract from Bradshaw's Guide for 1866. (Reprinted by Middleton Press 2011)

79. This view is of Roxburgh facing Tweedmouth, with the Jedburgh branch diverging to the right. It was taken level with the signal box, on 6th September 1955. (H.C.Casserley)

80. We are facing towards Tweedmouth on 14th April 1963 with the coaches of the 'Scottish Rambler No.2' in the island platform while the locomotive prepares to run around the train. (R.M.Casserley)

81. Class V1 2-6-2T no. 67617 pauses in the station before departing for Kelso with its one coach train, in the 1950s. (N.E.Stead.coll)

82.   Excursions to the Royal Highland Show at Kelso brought long trains and more unusual locomotives to the junction. Examples of V2, B1, D1 and D30 have been recorded. Here class D11 4-4-0 no. 62687 *Lord James of Douglas* has a Hawick train on 19th June 1952. (C.J.B.Sanderson/ARPT)

83.   The RCTS Borders Railtour is ready to leave for Tweedmouth on 9th July 1961. It is seen here from the Jedburgh branch looking back towards the station. In charge of the train are class D34 4-4-0 no. 256 *Glen Douglas* in NBR livery and class J37 0-6-0 no. 64624. (G.W.Morrison)

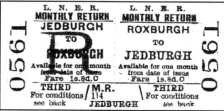

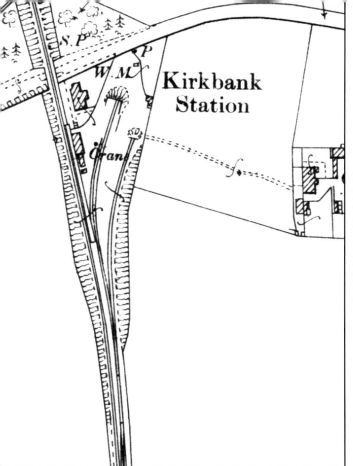

Jedburgh Branch
KIRKBANK

XXI. The 1898 survey is sadly poor quality. The first station on the Jedburgh branch originally opened on 17th July 1856 as Old Ormiston but was renamed Kirkbank on 20th May 1868. It temporarily closed to passengers on 13th August 1948 due to the extensive flooding in the Borders but never reopened. It became an unstaffed public siding on 1st July 1959 before closing completely on 10th August 1964.

The finger sign no longer directs passengers to the station which today is a private house. It was photographed on 25th June 2011. (A.E.Young)

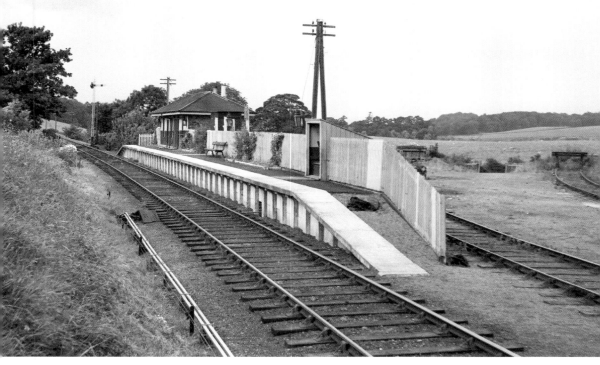

84.	The station looks smart with the concrete facings to the platform and repairs to the fence in this photograph taken on 14th July 1952. (N.E.Stead coll.)

85.	Class D34 4-4-0 no. 62471 *Glen Falloch* was at Kirkbank station with the Branch Line Society's 'Scott Country' Railtour on 4th April 1959. (R.Barbour/R.B.McCartney coll.)

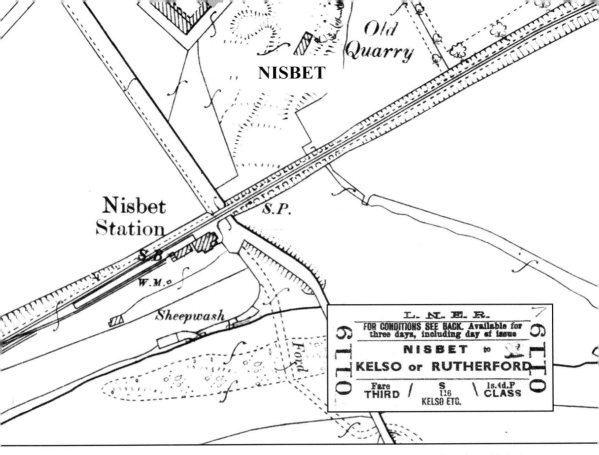

XXII. Nisbet opened on 17th July 1856 and remained in use until it was closed on 13th August 1948 when flooding caused major disruption in the area and temporarily closed many lines. It reopened to goods traffic becoming an unstaffed public siding on 1st June 1960. It closed outright on 10th August 1964 and is shown on the 1898 edition.

The centre of Nisbet was quiet on 24th June 2013. (D.A.Lovett)

86.   The station at Nisbet also served as the local post office (notice the sign above the door of the station master's house). This view is towards Jedburgh on 14th July 1952. (N.E.Stead coll.)

87.   There was provision for one siding and a headshunt behind the platform fence. In the background is a metal 'Bailey Bridge' over the local stream. Built after the 1948 floods, it was still there in 2014. (R.W.Lynn coll.)

JEDFOOT

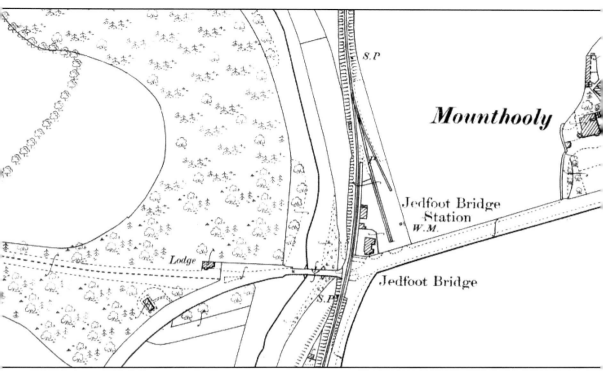

XXIII. The 1898 issue is at 40ins to 1 mile. Opened with the branch on 17th July 1856 it was named Jedfoot Bridge before being renamed Jedfoot in 1913. It lost its passenger services on 13th August 1948 before finally losing its modest goods facilities on 10th August 1964.

This blue enamel North British sign was still warning would be trespassers on 27th June 1962, nearly 40 years after the company ceased to exist. (R.R.Darsley)

88.	We are looking towards Jedburgh in the 1930s. Note the grounded van body providing extra storage. Otherwise the station house is similar to those already passed on the branch. (LOSA)

89.	On 27th June 1962 the station was unchanged but the station was boarded up and the goods yard was a dumping area for oil tanks. (R.R.Darsley)

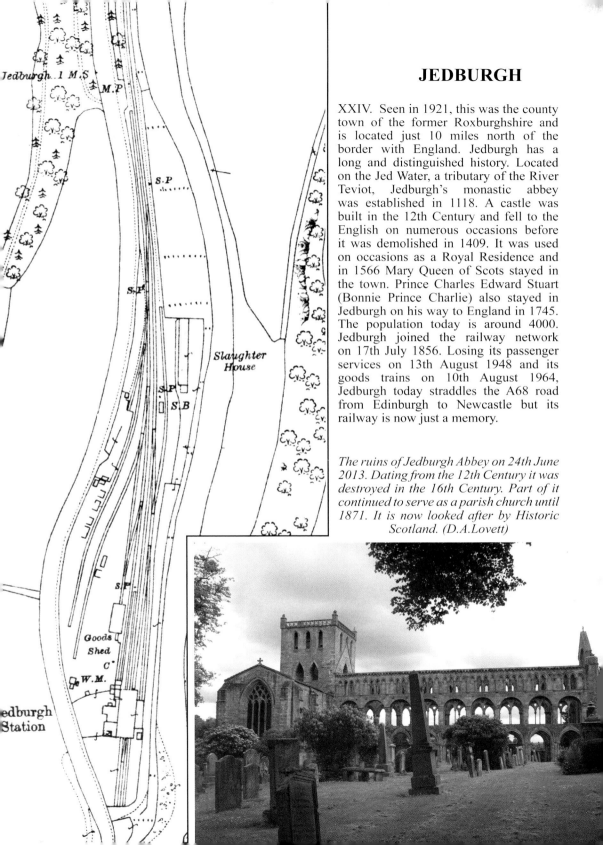

Jedburgh 1 M.S

M.P

S.P

S.P

Slaughter
House

S.P

S.B

S.P

Goods
Shed

C°

W.M.

edburgh
Station

JEDBURGH

XXIV. Seen in 1921, this was the county town of the former Roxburghshire and is located just 10 miles north of the border with England. Jedburgh has a long and distinguished history. Located on the Jed Water, a tributary of the River Teviot, Jedburgh's monastic abbey was established in 1118. A castle was built in the 12th Century and fell to the English on numerous occasions before it was demolished in 1409. It was used on occasions as a Royal Residence and in 1566 Mary Queen of Scots stayed in the town. Prince Charles Edward Stuart (Bonnie Prince Charlie) also stayed in Jedburgh on his way to England in 1745. The population today is around 4000. Jedburgh joined the railway network on 17th July 1856. Losing its passenger services on 13th August 1948 and its goods trains on 10th August 1964, Jedburgh today straddles the A68 road from Edinburgh to Newcastle but its railway is now just a memory.

The ruins of Jedburgh Abbey on 24th June 2013. Dating from the 12th Century it was destroyed in the 16th Century. Part of it continued to serve as a parish church until 1871. It is now looked after by Historic Scotland. (D.A.Lovett)

90. We are looking south towards the town in the 1930s. The station had its overall roof still, with the one road engine shed on the left. (LOSA)

91. The overall roof has gone though the engine shed is just behind the retaining wall. This is still in LNER days and a class J36 0-6-0 is running around its train. (N.E.Stead coll.)

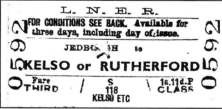

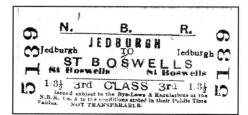

Extract from Bradshaw's Guide for 1866.
(Reprinted by Middleton Press 2011)

92.   The engine shed, on the left, opened with the line on the 17th June 1856 and closed on 2nd April 1949. Branch line motive power was supplied thereafter by St. Boswells shed. The goods shed is on the right.(N.E.Stead coll.)

93.   Jedburgh had a very fine signal box here photographed about 1961-2. This was the communications centre on the day of the 1948 floods. Mr. Bennett, the Station Master, noted there was a passenger train in the station when the alarm was raised. The locomotive was despatched up the line to see how bad it was. On its return, passengers were sent home by taxi and the passenger service was no more. (R.S.Carpenter)

KELSO, ROXBURGH, and JEDBURGH.

Miles	Down.	Week Days only.							Miles	Up.	Week Days only.						
		mrn	mrn	S	aft	aft	aft	aft	S			mrn	mrn	S	aft	aft	aft	aft	S
	Kelso............dep.	8 40	1112	1215	3 21	4 14	6 27	..	8 55		Jedburgh........dep.	7 15	9 57	12 6	1 50	4 1	5 50	7 6	8 15
3	Roxburgh......{ arr.	8 46	1128	1220	3 26	4 19	6 32	..	9 0	1¾	Jedfoot...........	7 20	10 1	..	1 54	4 5	5 54	7 10	8 19
	{ dep.	9 0	1139	1 32	3 32	4 23	6 35	7 30	9 8	2¼	Nisbet.............	7 24	10 4	1211	1 57	4 8	5 59	7 13	8 23
4¼	Kirkbank...........	9 5	1143	..	3 38	4 27	6 39	7 34	9 12	5¼	Kirkbank.........	7 32	1010	..	2 3	4 14	6 5	7 19	8 29
7¼	Nisbet...............	9 12	1149	1 40	3 44	4 33	6 45	7 40	9 18	7	Roxburgh 986..{ arr.	7 36	1014	1219	2 7	4 18	6 9	7 23	8 33
8½	Jedfoot.............	9 16	1153	..	3 48	4 37	6 49	7 44	9 22		{ dep.	7 47	1022	1 31	2 18	..	6 13	7 26	8 41
10	Jedburgh........arr.	9 21	1158	1 46	3 53	4 42	6 54	7 49	9 27	10	Kelso 936........arr.	7 52	1027	1 36	2 23	..	6 18	7 31	8 46

S Sats. only.   **OTHER TRAINS** between Kelso and Roxburgh, page 986.

1935 Jedburgh branch timetable.

94. The former station site was replaced by an industrial estate when it was visited on 25th June 2011. (A.E.Young)

JEDBURGH BRANCH
DOWN TRAINS — WEEKDAYS

No.	362		337	759	363		760	338	339	340		
Description	OP		OP		OP			OP	Mxd. OP	OP		
Class				D			D					
Departs from									Alternate Saturdays			

Distance from Jedburgh — M. C.

				HC am	SO PM	HC PM		SX PM	HC PM	PM	HC PM		
Jedburgh .... (S)	7 0		...	9 57	12 35	1 48		3 0	5 30	5 30	...	7 25	...
1 55 Jedfoot	7 4		10 1	...	1 52		...	5 34	5 35	...	7 29	...
2 71 Nisbet	7 7		10 4	...	1 55		...	5 38	5 39	...	7 32	...
5 36 Kirkbank	7 13		10 10	...	2 1		...	5 44	5 47	...	7 38	...
7 8 Roxburgh Junction .. (S)	7 17		10 14	1 5	2 5		3 30	5 48	5 51	...	7 42	...

Arrives at	Kelso 7.30 a.m.		Kelso 1.52 p.m.	Berwick			Kelso 3.58 p.m.	Kelso 6.1 p.m.				
Forward Times on Page	W96			W96	W96		W96	W96				

No. 337—Does not convey empty Coaching Stock.
No. 338—On alternate Saturdays will be Mixed, and run as shown in No. 339.

Working timetable for the branch 23rd May to 25th September 1948.

JEDBURGH BRANCH
UP TRAINS — WEEKDAYS

No.	364	514	366		519		365	367	368	369	369		
Description	Mxd. OP		OP				OP	Mxd. OP	OP	OP	Mxd. OP		
Class		D			D								
Departs from	Kelso 8.40 a.m.	St. Boswells 9.20 a.m.			St. Boswells 10.30 a.m.		Kelso 4.30 p.m.		Kelso 6.47 p.m.				

Distance from Roxburgh Junction — M. C.

	am	SO am	am		SX PM		PM	PM	PM	PM	PM		
Roxburgh Junction .. (S)	9 0	10 30	11F59		12 20		4 41	4 49	6 59	8 13	8F13	...
1 52 Kirkbank	9 5	10 43	12F 9		12 41		4 45	4 54	7 3	8 17	8F18	...
4 17 Nisbet	9 12	10 58	12F 9		1 8		4 51	5 1	7 9	8 23	8F25	...
5 33 Jedfoot	9 16	11 8	12F13		1 28		4 55	5 5	7 13	8 27	8F29	...
7 8 Jedburgh .... (S)	9 21	11 17	12F18		1 35		5 0	5 10	7 18	8 32	8F34	...

Horse Box traffic for Jedfoot to be taken to Jedburgh and returned by first train.
No. 364—Does not lift or leave wagons at Jedfoot. Conveys Live Stock from Roxburgh for Nisbet and Jedburgh, and when Stock is conveyed for Nisbet and Jedburgh, the train will arrive Jedburgh ten minutes later.
Nos. 514 and 519—Work back 3.0 p.m. S X (12.35 p.m. S O), Jedburgh to St. Boswells, via Kelso.

No. 366—F Will leave Roxburgh at 12.1 and run correspondingly later if Van traffic heavy.
No. 365—When train is Mixed, will run as shown in No. 367.
No. 369—Two minutes later on Saturdays. When train is Mixed, will run as shown in next column.
No. 369—F Two minutes later on Saturdays.

This timetable was in use at the time of the August 1948 floods.

DUNION QUARRY

There have been only three industrial railway sites in the whole of Roxburghshire; Dunion Quarry, two and a half miles south west of Jedburgh, the Charlesfield Armaments Depot which will be covered in photographs 103-105, and the Forestry Commission at Newcastleton which is mentioned in our Carlisle to Hawick album.

Dunion Hill, at 1092ft, is the north east summit of Black Law. It has a pre-historic fort, a ruined watch tower and a large quarry. Access to the quarry was from the B6358 road. The quarry had been worked before 1890 but there is no evidence from maps that railway track was used in the quarry before 1921. The last private owner was John Miller & Co., Contractors of North Queensferry, Fife. Roxburghshire County Council took over the quarry and two 4wPM locomotives were supplied to the quarry by Lister (their no. 6988 of 1935 and no. 9255 of 1937). These were 2ft gauge and suitable for hauling tip wagons from the rock face to the crusher. At a later date a 4wDM built by Motor Rail as no. 7171 of 1937 was acquired by the Council, second hand from the Wye River Board at Hereford. It is likely that the rail system closed in the early 1960s as there is no evidence of the rail system on 1960s maps and no evidence of the locomotives disposal.

Roxburgh Estates Forest Tramway

While seeking information on Dunion Hill, we were diverted to an early 20th century paper of the Transactions of the Royal Scottish Agricultural Society where the benefits of a horse drawn forest tramway from the felling area to the sawmill in the days before the arrival of motor traffic. A similar tramway but using two 4wDM Hunslet locomotives (no. 2024/5 of 1940) was used in the forests around Newcastleton.

Military Specials to Jedburgh

This is part of the Special Train Notices for Saturday 15th July 1922. Jedburgh was used to get soldiers to Otterburn Ranges when the normal access point through Woodburn on the NBR Wansbeck Valley line was already congested.

Other unusual workings

From July 1932 to March 1941 the Sentinel 6 cylinder steam railcar *Royal Charlotte* worked from Berwick to Coldstream and Kelso, based at Tweedmouth.

A class D20 4-4-0 from Tweedmouth stayed overnight at Jedburgh in a post war timetable that saw a crew exchange trains at Twizell. A Heaton class C7 4-4-2 worked on Saturdays from Newcastle to Berwick, Tweedmouth to Coldstream and return until the class was withdrawn.

Perhaps the most unusual recorded working was Jubilee Class 4-6-0 no. 45696 *Arethusa* which worked a 'fill in' freight to Jedburgh on 29th May 1964.

75	Special Mixed Military Train—Barry Links to Jedburgh.						
			a.m.				a.m.
Dundee (empty)	...	depart	3 30	Dalmeny ...	...	pass	7 47
Barry Links	...	depart	5 20	Haymarket West	...	,,	8 5
Broughty Ferry	...	pass	5 34	Niddrie West	...	arrive	8 20
Camperdown Junction	...	,,	5 42	Do.	...	depart	8 35
Dundee (Tay Bridge)	...	arrive	5 46	Niddrie South	...	pass	8 40
Do.	...	depart	5 52	Hardengreen	...	,,	8 50
Tay Bridge South	...	pass	6 2	Falahill ...	...	,,	9 20
Leuchars ...	...	,,	6 14	Galashiels	...	,,	9 55
Ladybank	...	,,	6 40	St Boswells	...	arrive	10 13
Thornton ...	...	,,	6 58	Do.	...	depart	10 18
Kirkcaldy	...	,,	7 9	Roxburgh Junction	...	pass	10 40
Burntisland	...	,,	7 21	Jedburgh ...	...	arrive	10 56
Inverkeithing	...	,,	7 36				
Forth Bridge North	...	,,	7 42	Empty to St Boswells.			

Conveys 130 horses in 19 cattle trucks.

76	Special Military Train—Aberdeen to Jedburgh.						
			a.m.				p.m.
Aberdeen ...	...	depart	9 0	Burntisland	...	pass	12 3
Stonehaven	...	pass	9 25	Inverkeithing	...	arrive	12 13
Kinnaber Junction	...	,,	9 54	Do.	...	depart	12 20
Montrose ...	...	arrive	9 58	Forth Bridge North	...	pass	12 23
Do.	...	depart	10 3	Dalmeny ...	...	,,	12 28
Usan	...	,,	10 21	Haymarket West Junct.	...	,,	12 38
Inverkeilor	...	,,	10 30	Niddrie West	...	arrive	12 W50
St Vigeans Junction	...	pass	10 38	Do.	...	depart	12 55
Arbroath ...	...	,,	10 39	Niddrie South	...	pass	12 58
Broughty Ferry	...	,,	10 54	St Boswells	...	arrive	1 51
Dundee (Tay Bridge)	...	,,	11 4	Do.	...	depart	1 56
Leuchars Junction	...	,,	11 18	Roxburgh Junction	...	pass	2 18
Ladybank ...	...	,,	11 33	Jedburgh ...	...	arrive	2 38
Thornton ...	...	,,	11 47	Empty to Craigentinny.			

Conveys 75th Brigade R.F.A. 30 men. 13 horses in horse boxes. 1 van baggage.

RUTHERFORD

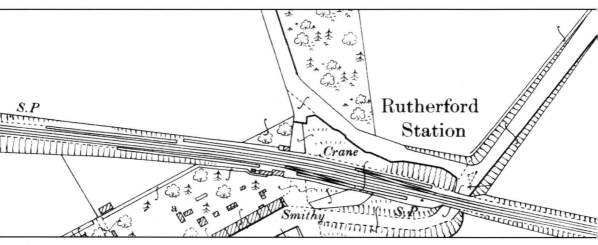

XXV. This is the 25ins scale map from 1898. Opened on 17th June 1850, Rutherford served a rural community. Although built as double track, on Sunday 5th November 1933 the line from St. Boswells (Kelso Junction) to Kelso was singled. On 2nd November 1959 it became an unstaffed halt and public delivery siding. It closed to goods on 18th May 1964 and to passengers shortly afterwards on 15th June 1964.

Station lamp and sign.
(Colour-Rail.com)

This view on 24th June 2013 is of every residence in Rutherford. The station was off to the right and the railway ran behind the houses. (D.A.Lovett)

95. The station comprised a small brick office and shelter with a coach body as a store. The buildings were in the goods yard with the platform further west. (Colour-Rail.com)

96. Looking towards Kelso we can see the road under-bridge parapets in the distance. The platform was of modest construction to serve the small rural community but the yard was originally equipped with a crane and two sidings. (Colour-Rail.com)

97.　Looking towards St. Boswells, we get a better view of the office and the smart platform with its white washed steps. When the line was singled in 1933, the up platform, which was beyond the end of the siding on the right, was removed. (R.W.Lynn coll.)

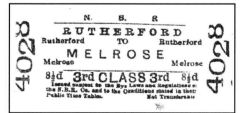

MAXTON

Maxton station totem. (R.B.McCartney)

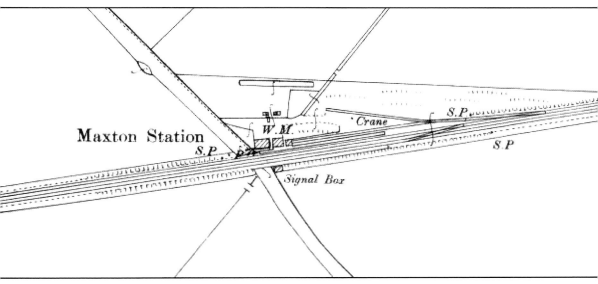

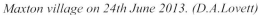

XXVI. This is the 1898 survey. It opened on 17th June 1850 and closed to passengers on 15th June 1964, becoming an unstaffed public siding on the same day. Goods traffic continued until 25th January 1965.

Maxton village on 24th June 2013. (D.A.Lovett)

98.   C15 class 4-4-2T no. 9039 (later BR no. 67477) arrives with a train for St. Boswells in LNER days, possibly 1937. (I.R.Smith/R.W.Lynn coll.)

99.   Looking east from the level crossing, we get a better view of the station building and part of the station house. The Maxton loop was reinstated when Charlesfield Armaments factory opened in 1942. (R.W.Lynn coll.)

100.   Class J39 0-6-0 no. 64917 runs through with the daily Tweedmouth - St.Boswells freight on 26th August 1960. Note the wartime austerity sleepering with concrete bosses between regular sleepers, used when the station loop was reinstated in 1942. (H. Ballantyne/Rail Photoprints)

101.   BR 2MT 2-6-0 no. 78048 leaves Maxton with the 14.21 from Kelso to St. Boswells on 26th August 1960. (H. Ballantyne/Rail Photoprints)

102.   The gates are opened for the final freight to Kelso in March 1968. The station buildings and signal box have already been demolished and the loop removed again when the line became freight only. (R.B.McCartney)

Down working timetable for the Kelso to St. Boxwells line in Summer 1949.

KELSO BRANCH

DOWN TRAINS — **WEEKDAYS**

No.	219	364	225	233	238	239	759	365	248	760	253	89	259
Description	OP	OP	OP	OP	OP	OP		OP	OP		OP	OP	OP
Class							D			D			
Departs from							Jedburgh 12.35 p.m.			Roxburgh 3.48 p.m.			
M. C.	am	HC am	HC am	SO HC PM	SO HC PM	SX HC PM	SO PM	PM	HC PM	SX PM	HC PM	PM	HC PM
Kelso .... (T)	7 40	8 40	10 20	12 9	2 0	2 20	2 20	4 30	4 40	4 50	6 22	6 47	8 5 ....
2 36 Heiton ..	..	..	..	..	..	..	..	..	..	..	..	..	..
2 78 Roxburgh Junction .. (T)	7 47	8 46	10 27	12 15	2 7	2 27	2 30	4 36	4 47	4 58	6 29	6 53	8 11 ....
6 3 Roxburgh Junction (T)	7 48	9 0	10 28	12 16	2 9	2 29	2 55	..	4 49	5 10	6 35	6 59	8 13 ..
Rutherford	7 55	..	10 35	12 23	2 15	2 35	..	..	4 55	5 25	..	..	8 20 ..
8 45 Maxton .. .. (T)	8 0	..	10 40	..	2 20	2 40	..	..	5 0	5 44	6 45	..	8 25 ..
11 46 St. Boswells ......(T)	8 6	..	10 46	12 33	2 26	2 46	3 25	..	5 6	5 55	6 51	..	8 31 ..
Arrives at		Jedburgh 9.21 a.m.			Galashiels 2.43 p.m.				Jedburgh 5.0 p.m.		Jedburgh 7.18 p.m.		
Forward Times on Page	W96				W39				W96		W96		

No. 225—Does not convey empty Coaching Vehicles.
No. 253— When Braked Goods traffic is lifted at Roxburgh Junction, will run three minutes later.

No. 259—Conveys only traffic, Kelso to St. Boswells.

CHARLESFIELD

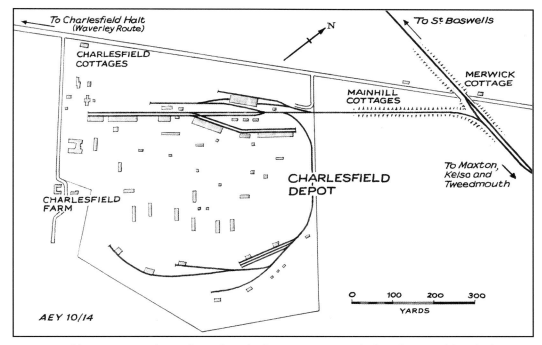

XXVII. This map was redrawn from the sale document prepared after closure of the site in 1961. The factory had served as a Munitions Factory during 1942, closing in 1945 and then passing to the Royal Navy in 1949 to serve as an armaments depot. It was purchased by West Cumberland Farmers in December 1963 from the Ministry of Defence. The loop near Merwick Cottage was added purely for Charlesfield traffic in 1942, after the line had been singled in 1933. The site covered over 168 acres and encompassed 5090 yards of single track, a 30T railway weighbridge and an 18ft x 8ft straight platform. (A.E.Young)

103. A rare picture of some of the factory workers employed at Charlesfield during World War II. (R.B.McCartney coll.)

104.   Staff pose at Charlesfield with no. 1 0-4-0DM AB 366 1943 which served at the site from 1943 until 1950. It was replaced by 4wDM RH 221562/1944 which arrived from RNAD Ditton Priors, Shropshire in 1950 and departed to RNSD, Dalmeny, Kirkliston, West Lothian around May 1961. (R.W.Lynn coll.)

Charlesfield was served by a passenger halt on the Waverley route. See our *Hawick to Galashiels* album for additional information and photographs.

105.   This aerial photograph is looking to the north, and is one of a series held by the Royal Commission on the Ancient and Historical Monuments of Scotland. [Published under Licence]

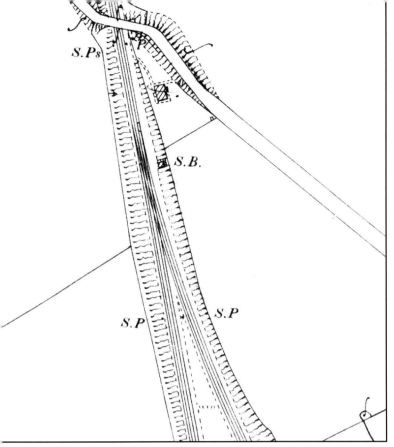

S.Ps

S.B.

S.P   S.P

KELSO JUNCTION

XXVIII. This is where the Kelso branch joined the Waverley Route, south of St. Boswells and was surveyed in 1921.

Up working timetable for the St. Boswells - Kelso line in Summer 1949

KELSO BRANCH

			244	362	248	514	519	254	265	759	363	760	278	376	269	286
	UP TRAINS	**WEEKDAYS**														
	No.		244	362	248	514	519	254	265	759	363	760	278	376	269	286
	Description		OP	OP	OP			OP	OP		OP		OP	OP	OP	OP
	Class					D	D				D		D				
	Departs from		Jedburgh 7.0 a.m.							Jedburgh 12.35 p.m.	Jedburgh 1.48 p.m.	Jedburgh 3.0 p.m.		Jedburgh 5.30 p.m.		
M. C.			am	am	am	SO am	SX am	am	SO PM	SO PM	PM	SX PM	PM	PM	PM	PM
	St. Boswells ......(T)..		6 18	.....	8 37	9 20	10 30	11 35	1 28	.....	.....	.....	4 0	.....	6 17	7 25
3 1	Maxton .. (T)..		..	..	8 43	9 33	11 5	11 41	1 34	..	..	..	4 6	..	6 23	7 31
5 43	Rutherford		AA	....	8 48	9 46	11 25	11 46	1 39	..	..	..	4 11	..	6 28	7 36
8 48	Roxburgh Junction (T)..		6 32	7 17	8 54	9 56	11 35	11 52	1 44	..	2 5	..	4 16	5 48	6 33	7 41
	Roxburgh Junction ..(T)..		6 36	7 24	8 55	.....	12 20	11 54	1 45	1 51	2 13	3 48	4 18	5 55	6F35	7 45
11 46	Kelso ..(T)..		6 41	7 30	9 0	..	..	11 59	1 50	2 1	2 18	3 58	4 23	6 1	6F40	7 50
	Arrives at			Jedburgh 11.17 a.m.	Jedburgh 1.35 p.m.										Jedburgh 7.18 p.m.	
	Forward Times on Page					W96	W96								W97	

No. 244—AA Calls at Rutherford when required to set down workmen.

No. 269—F Runs three minutes later when vehicles are attached at Roxburgh Junction.

106.   The last freight from Kelso is held at Kelso Junction on 29th March 1968 while a northbound train passes on the Waverley route. Locomotive no. D3891 is carrying the unofficial Kelso Lad headboard made by Ian Fergusson. (R.B.McCartney)

107.   A class 40 heads south past Kelso Junction with a Millerhill to Kingmoor freight on 29th March 1968, while the last local pickup from Kelso waits to join the main line and head north. The Kelso Junction signal box had been replaced by a ground frame. (R.B.McCartney)

ST BOSWELLS ENGINE SHED

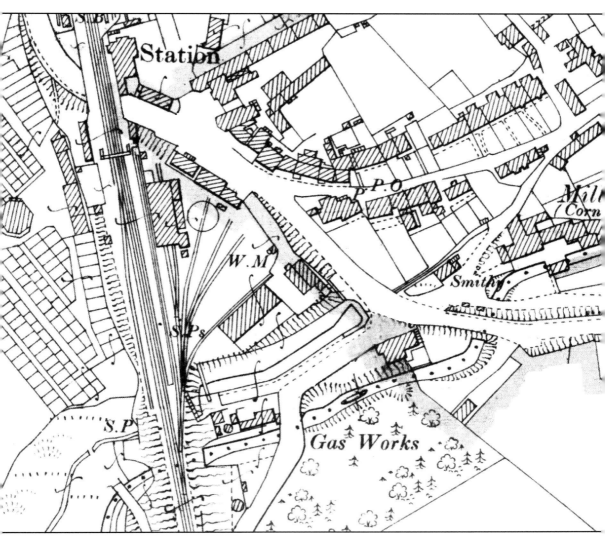

XXIX. The area is on the 1921 edition. The first shed opened north of the station on 20th February 1849. It was replaced by a new facility in January 1863 adjacent to the station. It closed as a sub-shed of Hawick on 16th November 1959 and thereafter locomotives were provided by Hawick shed. The building survives in industrial use, although all traces of the station itself are long gone

For further pictures of St. Boswells shed see our
Hawick to Galashiels **and**
St. Boswells to Berwick via Duns albums.

108.   The shed, on the right, was integral to the station and the bay platform running along the shed wall was the normal departure platform for trains to Kelso and Berwick. (R.W.Lynn coll.)

109.   Class G5 0-4-4-T no. 67268 waits on a Kelso train while J36 class 0-6-0 no. 65331 has just coaled up. The J36 has a tender cab for reverse working. (R.W.Lynn coll.)

110.   Prominent in this photograph are two class D30 4-4-0s, no. 62440 *Wandering Willie* and no. 62423 *Dugald Dalgetty*. The other locomotive is a J35 class 0-6-0. (N.E.Stead coll.)

111.   There is less steam and smoke in this 1955 view so we have a clearer view of the shed, water tank and coaling stage. The locomotives are a J35 class 0-6-0 and another 'Scott' class 4-4-0. (Photos of the 50s)

ST. BOSWELLS

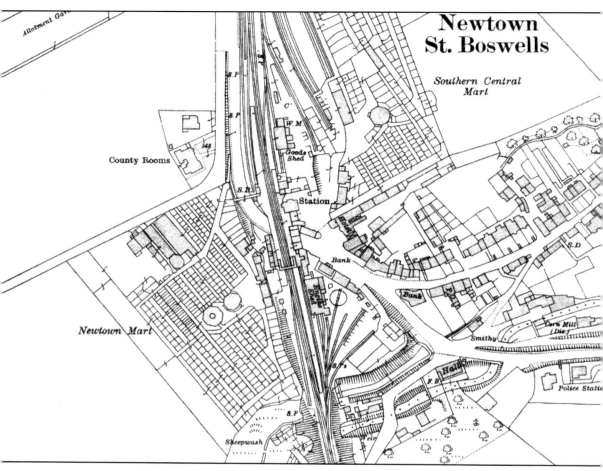

XXX. St. Boswells in 1908. The extension of the Edinburgh & Dalkeith Railway south towards Hawick saw the arrival of what was to become the Waverley route into the area. Local landowners ensured that the railway was kept out of the picturesque village of St. Boswells itself, which often hosts the Buccleuch Hunt on the village green. It resulted in the railway establishing itself in the nearby community of Newtown St. Boswells, a mile away, which resulted in the development of a livestock market. It became the administrative centre for Roxburghshire and in 1975 its successor the Borders Regional Council, now the Scottish Borders Council. Opened as Newtown Junction on 1st November 1849, it was renamed New Town St. Boswells in January 1863 before becoming St. Boswells in March 1865. Over the years it saw the opening of two cross country routes to Berwick, one on either bank of the River Tweed. Whilst the Kelso route is the subject of this album, the other line via Duns opened as a through route on 16th November 1863 before flooding forced its closure on 13th August 1948. The middle section was not restored but the two ends eventually reopened. The western end of the line remained open as far as Greenlaw for goods traffic before closing on 19th July 1965. The album for the line via Duns was published by Middleton Press in 2013. St. Boswells finally lost its passenger services with closure of the Waverley Route on 6th January 1969 and its goods services on 25th April 1969.

112.   NBR 0-6-0 no. 195 was built by Dubs in 1866. It was renumbered to no. 1051 in 1908 and was still running in 1922. This is an official photograph of the station and behind the train is the original standard NBR footbridge. (R.M.Casserley coll.)

113.   Another official photograph from the other end of the platform includes the covered in footbridge and platform awnings. (Clapperton Trust)

114.   D30 class 4-4-0 no. 62423 *Dugald Dalgetty* waits with a Berwick train via Kelso in the south bay on 18th July 1953. (Colour-Rail.com)

115.   K3 class 2-6-0 no. 61983 with a northbound goods train is seen here on 18th September 1957. (M.J.Reade/Colour-Rail.com)

116.   North Eastern Railway locomotives did operate the branch in BR days but they were usually class G5 0-4-4T. Class D20 4-4-0 no. 62383 normally operated between Newcastle and Alnwick. (N.E.Stead.coll)

117.   Quite a crowd has gathered by the South signal box for the arrival of the Edinburgh bound 'Waverley' hauled by A3 class 4-6-2 no. 60093 *Cornach*. The first A3 to do this run through from Leeds was in 1954 but it was 1960 before it was a regular turn. (J.Parker/Photos of the 50s)

118.   The Kelso branch train is a two coach train with a class V1 2-6-2T at its head. Between 1956 and 1959 no. 67606 was the regular locomotive on the branch. (D.Lawrence/Photos of the 50s)

119.   A1 Class 4-6-2 no. 60152 *Holyrood* takes water whilst working an early morning Waverley Route service in January 1962. (D.Cobbe/Rail Photoprints)

120.   A bus stops opposite the station hotel at Newtown St. Boswells on 24th June 2012. The retaining wall on the right supported the remains of the railway embankment and indicates where the railway crossed over the road to reach the station. (D.A.Lovett)

> **For further pictures of St. Boswells shed see our *Hawick to Galashiels* and *St. Boswells to Berwick via Duns* albums.**

The station name board gives an indication of its once strategic importance on the Border railway network. Seen here in 1955 after the loss of the St. Boswells to Berwick via Duns line and the closure of the Jedburgh branch to passenger trains. (B.Connell/Photos of the 50s)

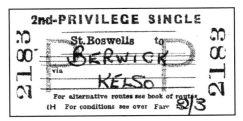

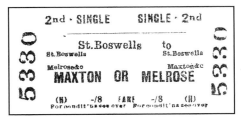

MP Middleton Press

EVOLVING THE ULTIMATE RAIL ENCYCLOPEDIA

Easebourne Midhurst GU29 9AZ. Tel:01730 813169

www.middletonpress.co.uk email:info@middletonpress.co.uk

A-978 0 906520 B- 978 1 873793 C- 978 1 901706 D-978 1 904474 E - 978 1 906008 F - 978 1 908174

All titles listed below were in print at time of publication - please check current availability by looking at our website - *www.middletonpress.co.uk* or by requesting a Brochure which includes our *LATEST* RAILWAY TITLES also our TRAMWAY, TROLLEYBUS, MILITARY and COASTAL series

A

Abergavenny to Merthyr C 91 8
Abertillery & Ebbw Vale Lines D 84 5
Aberystwyth to Carmarthen E 90 1
Allhallows - Branch Line to A 62 8
Alton - Branch Lines to A 11 6
Andover to Southampton A 82 6
Ascot - Branch Lines around A 64 2
Ashburton - Branch Line to B 95 4
Ashford - Steam to Eurostar B 67 1
Ashford to Dover A 48 2
Austrian Narrow Gauge D 04 3
Avonmouth - BL around D 42 5
Aylesbury to Rugby D 91 3

B

Baker Street to Uxbridge D 90 6
Bala to Llandudno E 87 1
Banbury to Birmingham D 27 2
Banbury to Cheltenham E 63 5
Bangor to Holyhead F 01 7
Bangor to Portmadoc E 72 7
Barking to Southend C 80 2
Barmouth to Pwllheli E 53 6
Barry - Branch Lines around D 50 0
Bartlow - Branch Lines to F 27 7
Bath Green Park to Bristol C 36 9
Bath to Evercreech Junction A 60 4
Beamish 40 years on rails E94 9
Bedford to Wellingborough D 31 9
Berwick to Drem F 64 2
Berwick to St. Boswells F 75 8
B'ham to Tamworth & Nuneaton F 63 5
Birkenhead to West Kirby F 61 1
Birmingham to Wolverhampton E253
Bletchley to Cambridge D 94 4
Bletchley to Rugby E 07 9
Bodmin - Branch Lines around B 83 1
Boston to Lincoln F 80 2
Bournemouth to Evercreech Jn A 46 8
Bournemouth to Weymouth A 57 4
Bradshaw's History F18 5
Bradshaw's Rail Times 1850 F 13 0
Bradshaw's Rail Times 1895 F 11 6
Branch Lines series - see town names
Brecon to Neath D 43 2
Brecon to Newport D 16 6
Brecon to Newtown E 06 2
Brighton to Eastbourne A 16 1
Brighton to Worthing A 03 1
Bristol to Taunton D 03 6
Bromley South to Rochester B 23 7
Bromsgrove to Birmingham D 87 6
Bromsgrove to Gloucester D 73 9
Broxbourne to Cambridge F16 1
Brunel - A railtour D 74 6
Bude - Branch Line to B 29 9
Burnham to Evercreech Jn B 68 0

C

Cambridge to Ely D 55 5
Canterbury - BLs around B 58 9
Cardiff to Dowlais (Cae Harris) E 47 5
Cardiff to Pontypridd E 95 6
Cardiff to Swansea E 42 0
Carlisle to Hawick E 85 7
Carmarthen to Fishguard E 66 6
Caterham & Tattenham Corner B251
Central & Southern Spain NG E 91 8
Chard and Yeovil - BLs a C 30 7
Charing Cross to Dartford A 75 8
Charing Cross to Orpington A 96 3
Cheddar - Branch Line to B 90 9
Cheltenham to Andover C 43 7
Cheltenham to Redditch D 81 4
Chester to Birkenhead F 21 5
Chester to Manchester F 51 2
Chester to Rhyl E 93 2
Chester to Warrington F 40 6
Chichester to Portsmouth A 14 7
Clacton and Walton - BLs to F 04 8
Clapham Jn to Beckenham Jn B 36 7
Cleobury Mortimer - BLs a E 18 5
Clevedon & Portishead - BLs to D180
Consett to South Shields E 57 4
Cornwall Narrow Gauge D 56 2
Corris and Vale of Rheidol E 65 9
Craven Arms to Llandeilo E 35 2
Craven Arms to Wellington E 33 8
Crawley to Littlehampton A 34 5
Crewe to Manchester F 57 4
Cromer - Branch Lines around C 26 0
Croydon to East Grinstead B 48 0
Crystal Palace & Catford Loop B 87 1
Cyprus Narrow Gauge E 13 0

D

Darjeeling Revisited F 09 3
Darlington Leamside Newcastle E 28 4
Darlington to Newcastle D 98 2
Dartford to Sittingbourne B 34 3
Denbigh - Branch Lines around F 32 1
Derwent Valley - BL to the D 06 7
Devon Narrow Gauge E 09 3
Didcot to Banbury D 02 9
Didcot to Swindon C 84 0
Didcot to Winchester C 13 0
Dorset & Somerset NG D 76 0
Douglas - Laxey - Ramsey E 75 8
Douglas to Peel C 88 8
Douglas to Port Erin C 55 0
Douglas to Ramsey D 39 5
Dover to Ramsgate A 78 9
Dublin Northwards in 1950s E 31 4
Dunstable - Branch Lines to E 27 7

E

Ealing to Slough C 42 0
Eastbourne to Hastings A 27 7
East Cornwall Mineral Railways D 22 7
East Croydon to Three Bridges A 53 6
Eastern Spain Narrow Gauge E 56 7
East Grinstead - BLs to A 07 9
East London - Branch Lines of C 44 4
East London Line B 80 0
East of Norwich - Branch Lines E 69 7
Effingham Junction - BLs a A 74 1
Ely to Norwich C 90 1
Enfield Town & Palace Gates D 32 6
Epsom to Horsham A 30 7
Eritrean Narrow Gauge E 38 3
Euston to Harrow & Wealdstone C 89 5
Exeter to Barnstaple B 15 2
Exeter to Newton Abbot C 49 9
Exeter to Tavistock B 69 5
Exmouth - Branch Lines to B 00 8

F

Fairford - Branch Line to A 52 9
Falmouth, Helston & St. Ives C 74 1
Fareham to Salisbury A 67 3
Faversham to Dover B 05 3
Felixstowe & Aldeburgh - BL to D 20 3
Fenchurch Street to Barking C 20 8
Festiniog - 50 yrs of enterprise C 83 3
Festiniog 1946-55 E 01 7
Festiniog in the Fifties B 68 8
Festiniog in the Sixties B 91 6
Ffestiniog in Colour 1955-82 F 25 3
Finsbury Park to Alexandra Pal C 02 8
Frome to Bristol B 77 0

G

Galashiels to Edinburgh F 52 9
Gloucester to Bristol D 35 7
Gloucester to Cardiff D 66 1
Gosport - Branch Lines around A 36 9
Greece Narrow Gauge D 72 2

H

Hampshire Narrow Gauge D 36 4
Harrow to Watford D 14 2
Harwich & Hadleigh - BLs to F 02 4
Harz Revisited F 62 8
Hastings to Ashford A 37 6
Hawick to Galashiels F 36 9
Hawkhurst - Branch Line to A 66 6
Hayling - Branch Line to A 12 3
Hay-on-Wye - BL around D 92 0
Haywards Heath to Seaford A 28 4
Hemel Hempstead - BLs to D 88 3
Henley, Windsor & Marlow - BLa C77 2
Hereford to Newport D 54 8
Hertford & Hatfield - BLs a E 58 1
Hertford Loop E 71 0
Hexham to Carlisle D 75 3
Hexham to Hawick F 08 6
Hitchin to Peterborough D 07 4
Holborn Viaduct to Lewisham A 81 9
Horsham - Branch Lines to A 02 4
Huntingdon - Branch Line to A 93 2

I

Ilford to Shenfield C 97 0
Ilfracombe - Branch Line to B 21 3
Industrial Rlys of the South East A 09 3
Ipswich to Diss F 81 9
Ipswich to Saxmundham C 41 3
Isle of Wight Lines - 50 yrs C 12 3
Italy Narrow Gauge F 17 8

K

Kent Narrow Gauge C 45 1
Kettering to Nottingham F 82-6
Kidderminster to Shrewsbury E 10 9
Kingsbridge - Branch Line to C 98 7
Kings Cross to Potters Bar E 62 8
King's Lynn to Hunstanton F 58 1
Kingston & Hounslow Loops A 83 3
Kingswear - Branch Line to C 17 8

L

Lambourn - Branch Line to C 70 3
Launceston & Princetown - BLs C 19 2
Lewisham to Dartford A 92 5
Lincoln to Cleethorpes F 56 7
Lines around Wimbledon B 75 6
Liverpool Street to Chingford D 01 2
Liverpool Street to Ilford C 34 5
Llandeilo to Swansea E 46 8
London Bridge to Addiscombe B 20 6
London Bridge to East Croydon A 58 1
Longmoor - Branch Lines to A 41 3
Looe - Branch Line to C 22 2
Loughborough to Nottingham F 68 0
Lowestoft - BLs around E 40 6
Ludlow to Hereford E 14 7
Lydney - Branch Lines around E 26 0
Lyme Regis - Branch Line to A 45 1
Lynton - Branch Line to B 04 6

M

Machynlleth to Barmouth E 54 3
Maesteg and Tondu Lines E 06 2
Majorca & Corsica Narrow Gauge F 41 3
March - Branch Lines around B 09 1
Market Drayton - BLs around F 67 3
Marylebone to Rickmansworth D 49 4
Melton Constable to Yarmouth Bch E031
Midhurst - Branch Lines of E 78 9
Midhurst - Branch Lines to F 00 0
Minehead - Branch Line to A 80 2
Mitcham Junction Lines B 01 5
Monmouth - Branch Lines to E 20 8
Monmouthshire Eastern Valleys D 71 5
Moretonhampstead - BL to C 27 7
Moreton-in-Marsh to Worcester D 26 5
Mountain Ash to Neath D 80 7

N

Newark to Doncaster F 78 9
Newbury to Westbury C 66 6
Newcastle to Hexham D 69 2
Newport (IOW) - Branch Lines to A 26 0
Newquay - Branch Lines to C 71 0
Newton Abbot to Plymouth C 60 4
Newtown to Aberystwyth E 41 3
North East German NG D 44 9
Northern Alpine Narrow Gauge F 37 6
Northern France Narrow Gauge C 75 8
Northern Spain Narrow Gauge E 83 3
North London Line B 94 7
North of Birmingham F 55 0
North Woolwich - BLs around C 65 9
Nottingham to Boston F 70 3
Nottingham to Lincoln F 43 7

O

Ongar - Branch Line to E 05 5
Orpington to Tonbridge B 03 9
Oswestry - Branch Lines around E 60 4
Oswestry to Whitchurch E 81 9
Oxford to Bletchley D 57 9
Oxford to Moreton-in-Marsh D 15 9

P

Paddington to Ealing C 37 6
Paddington to Princes Risborough C819
Padstow - Branch Line to B 54 1
Pembroke and Cardigan - BLs to F 29 1
Peterborough to Kings Lynn E 32 1
Peterborough to Newark F 72 7
Plymouth - BLs around B 98 5
Plymouth to St. Austell C 63 5
Pontypool to Mountain Ash D 65 4
Pontypridd to Merthyr F 14 7
Pontypridd to Port Talbot E 86 4
Porthmadog 1954-94 - BLa B 31 2
Portmadoc 1923-46 - BLa B 13 8
Portsmouth to Southampton A 31 4
Portugal Narrow Gauge E 67 3
Potters Bar to Cambridge D 70 8
Princes Risborough - BL to D 05 0
Princes Risborough to Banbury C 85 7

R

Railways to Victory C 16 1
Reading to Basingstoke B 27 5
Reading to Didcot C 79 6
Reading to Guildford A 47 5
Redhill to Ashford A 73 4
Return to Blaenau 1970-82 C 64 2
Rhyl to Bangor F 15 4
Rhymney & New Tredegar Lines E 48 2
Rickmansworth to Aylesbury D 61 6
Romania & Bulgaria NG E 23 9
Romneyrail C 32 1
Ross-on-Wye - BLs around E 30 7
Ruabon to Barmouth E 84 0
Rugby to Birmingham E 37 6
Rugby to Loughborough F 12 3
Rugby to Stafford F 07 9
Ryde to Ventnor A 19 2

S

Salisbury to Westbury B 39 8
Sardinia and Sicily Narrow Gauge F 50 5
Saxmundham to Yarmouth C 69 7
Saxony & Baltic Germany Revisited F 71 0
Saxony Narrow Gauge D 47 0
Seaton & Sidmouth - BLs to A 95 6
Selsey - Branch Line to A 04 8
Sheerness - Branch Line to B 16 2
Shenfield to Ipswich E 96 3
Shrewsbury - Branch Line to A 86 4
Shrewsbury to Chester E 70 3
Shrewsbury to Crewe F 48 2
Shrewsbury to Ludlow E 21 5
Shrewsbury to Newtown E 29 1
Sierra Leone Narrow Gauge D 28 9
Sirhowy Valley Line E 12 3
Sittingbourne to Ramsgate A 90 1
Skegness & Mablethorpe - BL to F 84 0
Slough to Newbury C 56 7
South African Two-foot gauge E 51 2
Southampton to Bournemouth A 42 0
Southend & Southminster BLs E 76 5
Southern Alpine Narrow Gauge F 22 2
Southern France Narrow Gauge C 47 5
South London Line B 46 6
South Lynn to Norwich City F 03 1
Southwold - Branch Line to A 15 4
Spalding - Branch Lines around E 52 9
Spalding to Grimsby F 65 9 6
Stafford to Chester F 34 5
Stafford to Wellington F 59 8
St Albans to Bedford D 08 1
St. Austell to Penzance C 67 3
St. Boswell to Berwick F 44 4
Steaming Through Isle of Wigh
Steaming Through West Hants
Stourbridge to Wolverhampton
St. Pancras to Barking D 68 5
St. Pancras to Folkestone E 88
St. Pancras to St. Albans C 78
Stratford to Cheshunt F 53 6
Stratford-u-Avon to Birminghar
Stratford-u-Avon to Cheltenhan
Sudbury - Branch Lines to F 19
Surrey Narrow Gauge C 87 1
Sussex Narrow Gauge C 68 0
Swanley to Ashford B 45 9
Swansea - Branch Lines aroun
Swansea to Carmarthen E 59 8
Swindon to Bristol C 96 3
Swindon to Gloucester D 46 3
Swindon to Newport D 30 2
Swiss Narrow Gauge C 94 9

T

Talyllyn 60 E 98 7
Tamworth to Derby F 76 5
Taunton to Barnstaple B 60 2
Taunton to Exeter C 82 6
Taunton to Minehead F 39 0
Tavistock to Plymouth B 88 6
Tenterden - Branch Line to A 21
Three Bridges to Brighton A 35
Tilbury Loop C 86 4
Tiverton - BLs around C 62 8
Tivetshall to Beccles D 41 8
Tonbridge to Hastings A 44 4
Torrington - Branch Lines to B 3
Towcester - BLs around E 39 0
Tunbridge Wells BLs A 32 1

U

Upwell - Branch Line to B 64 0

V

Victoria to Bromley South A 98
Victoria to East Croydon A 40 6
Vivarais Revisited E 08 6

W

Walsall Routes F 45 1
Wantage - Branch Line to D 25
Wareham to Swanage 50 yrs D
Waterloo to Windsor A 54 3
Waterloo to Woking A 38 3
Watford to Leighton Buzzard D 4
Wellingborough to Leicester F 7
Welshpool to Llanfair E 49 9
Wenford Bridge to Fowey C 09
Westbury to Bath B 55 8
Westbury to Taunton C 76 5
West Cornwall Mineral Rlys D 4
West Croydon to Epsom B 08 4
West German Narrow Gauge D
West London - BLs of C 50 5
West London Line B 84 8
West Wiltshire - BLs of D 12 8
Weymouth - BLs A 65 9
Willesden Jn to Richmond B 71
Wimbledon to Beckenham C 58
Wimbledon to Epsom B 62 6
Wimborne - BLs around A 97 0
Wisbech - BLs around C 01 7
Witham & Kelvedon - BLs a E 8
Woking to Alton A 59 8
Woking to Portsmouth A 25 3
Woking to Southampton A 55 0
Wolverhampton to Shrewsbury
Wolverhampton to Stafford F 79
Worcester to Birmingham D 97
Worcester to Hereford D 38 8
Worthing to Chichester A 06 2
Wrexham to New Brighton F 47
Wroxham - BLs around F 31 4

Y

Yeovil - 50 yrs change C 38 3
Yeovil to Dorchester A 76 5
Yeovil to Exeter A 91 8
York to Scarborough F 23 9